Developing Dynamic Disciples

Pentecostal Faith,

Prayer,

& Commitment

Developed and Edited by the
National Sunday School Promotion and Training
Department

Glen Percifield, Editor

GPH

Gospel Publishing House
Springfield, Missouri
02-0335

Library of Congress Catalog Card Number 94—76668
International Standard Book Number 0–88243–335–0
Printed in the United States of America

Contents

PROLOGUE

By Charles T. Crabtree
Assistant General Superintendent
Assemblies of God

"And what is your ministry in church?" I asked. With a noticeable droop of the shoulders and a defeatist monotone in the voice he answered, "Oh, I'm just a layman." Just one time, with the Lord's permission, I'd like to take a person who says those dreaded words by the shoulders and shake them awake to the fact they are playing into one of Satan's greatest traps; the trap of believing you have to be an ordained minister to have value and an effective ministry in the church of Jesus Christ.

The writer of the Hebrews mourns over those who ought to be teachers, but instead need to be taught the most elementary truth over and over again. They are like babies who can't be weaned (Hebrews 5:12, 13). They are the "high maintenance" Christians who have never understood their spiritual potential.

The future of the Pentecostal church in America depends to a great extent upon a spiritually revived laity who will believe God for a new anointing and a ministry with attending signs and wonders. We often plead for spiritual power; as we should, in the pulpit, but God wants to manifest His power as well through laymen whose pulpit is the corporate desk, the coffee table, or the Sunday school classroom.

You have been called by God to the Kingdom for such a time as this. A time of great spiritual apathy and biblical illiteracy. A time of moral drift and demonic activity. A time of abounding sin and pervasive evil. But it is also a time for revival and faith. A time for the supernatural and our Pentecostal witness. A time for holiness and righteousness. In short, we are living in the greatest time possible for God to use us all.

A lay leader in this culture must maintain certain priorities and characteristics if he or she is to be effective.

The effective lay minister must be totally committed.

This is no longer an option, it is a priority. The word *commitment* is not popular today. It might even scare some people away, but Kingdom work is all centered around commitment. Without a commitment we have no worthwhile ministry.

From the beginning, you must decide whether you are divinely called to a ministry. Do you know for certain it is God's will for you to be involved in the body of Christ? If the answer is yes, then the matter is no longer in your hands. The decision is obedience or rebellion.

The call of God to lay ministry is just as clear and just as vital as the call to full-time pulpit ministry. One should never resent divine direction, but glory in the privilege and potential of being led of God for a specific task.

If God has called you to a pulpit ministry, then it is incumbent upon you to make that ministry in and through the church a supreme priority, because you are answerable to God, not men.

Believe me, the work of the ministry is not always pleasant. God has not called us to a *party*, but to a ministry. There will be times of test and discouragement, but if God has called you, He will take all of it, the good and the bad, and make it into a masterpiece of eternal glory and reward.

The secret to maintaining an effective ministry is to keep the vision clear and the end result in focus. Jesus did. "Who for the joy that was set before him endured the cross, despising the shame, and is set down at the right hand of the throne of God" (Hebrews 12:2, KJV). Through the rigors of fulfilling your call, set the coming victory and joy before you. The process may not be easy, but the product is worth the effort.

Decide now to make your ministry a high priority. Commit to excellence. My mother taught me well. I can still hear her say, "Now, son, anything worth doing is worth doing well and things done in halves, are never done right." Commit to faithfulness. The Bible teaches that the responsibility of a steward is to be found faithful. I began my ministry as a choir director. I soon learned I would rather have a faithful "crow" than a spasmodic "nightingale." Above all, commit to God. Make all things in your life subject to His will. You are no longer your own. You are under new management.

The effective lay leader must be inner directed.

In other words, he must learn to live from the inside out, not the outside in. The kingdom of heaven is within. The outward man and all things around him are perishing, but the inward man is renewed day by day (2 Corinthians 4:16).

Many believers are being spiritually destroyed because they do not know how to handle the world around them, but as one wise old Christian said, "It's not the outward pressures that determine a Christian's life, but it is the inward braces."

We must have a Spirit-empowered laity who refuse to be pressed into the world's mold. The secret is in overcoming evil with good, by renewing the inner man with the Word of God and the mind of Christ.

If you are not careful, you will find yourself beginning the day offering unbelief, fear, and worry by taking in the news of the world around you. As a spiritual lay leader it is incumbent upon you to begin the day with the good news of the kingdom of God.

Build yourself up in the most holy faith day by day through the promises of God. Learn to see everything from God's point of view which is the result of having the mind of Christ. The advice of the prophet Isaiah is worth heeding, "Stop trusting in man, who has but a breath in his nostrils. Of what account is he?" (Isaiah 2:22). We are not born to a spirit of fear, "but of power, and of love, and of a sound mind" (2 Timothy 1:7, KJV).

Leadership does not begin through guiding others. It begins with the heart and discipline of the mind of the one who shall lead. That is the reason Jesus was so concerned about the heart and the mind. The lay minister who wants to be effective in today's world must live by inner faith and conviction.

The effective lay leader must be divinely taught.

How we need lay ministers and teachers who are so hungry to know God that they seek Him before they turn to books and materials about Him. Of course we are to study, striving for excellence. Whatever we do for God should be done with our whole body, soul, and mind, but we are to do these things in the power of the Spirit and not the energy of the flesh.

One of the greatest problems in the church today are teachers with carnal minds trying to convey spiritual truth. According to Romans 8:7, "The carnal mind is enmity against God" (KJV). It just cannot know the things of God.

What is a carnal mind? It is a mind filled with sensual knowledge and human wisdom. Often this kind of mind produces well structured lessons and appealing concepts, but the result is a lack of spiritual life both in the teacher and student.

No one believes in diligent study more than I, but I am constantly reminded that we can be ever learning, but never come to the knowledge of the truth (2 Timothy 3:7) and that "the letter killeth, but the Spirit giveth life" (2 Corinthians 3:6). It has been my sad experience to sit through Sunday school lessons taught by well read, knowledgeable people, but void of spiritual life and insight.

Remember, all the books (including this one), periodicals, tapes and articles are resources to help you, but your source is God. Without Him, all the resources are disconnected from divine power and will minister death, not life.

Before you study and while you study make certain your heart is humbled and your mind is open to the Spirit of God. Don't try to do anything in ministry whether it be preparation or delivery without seeking God and being aware of His presence.

Why is it so important to be divinely taught? Because those to whom you are going to minister are in desperate need of God whether they know it or not. It is our task to minister His life, His truth, and His power, not our own.

The Spirit-taught lay minister will be spiritually sensitive to the real needs of people. He or she will be able to take the truths they have studied from this book and others and make practical applications through divine revelation. He or she will not be bound to human wisdom and ability, but will be given supernatural authority to minister healing to the body, soul, and mind. Give us men and women in the Assemblies of God who are Spirit-filled, Spirit-led, and Spirit-taught.

You are a vital part of the kingdom of God. Don't ever say, "Oh, I'm just a layman," with a defeatist attitude again. You are a part of the greatest enterprise in the history of the world—the living, victorious church of Jesus Christ. Congratulations.

1

Spiritual Faith Formation

by Keith Heermann

In every civilization, someone has to put up the signs that
guide us on our way—proverb

Learning and reflecting on the process of our spiritual life
formation is a challenging task. In some ways the life of a
fruitful Christian is like the life of a fruit-laden tree. Break the
healthy roots of prayer, scriptural food, and vital connection
with Christ, and the Christian cannot bear fruit. Each person,
like each tree, is unique. Nourishment from the soil either
sustains or chokes the purpose and process of fruit bearing.

A non-spiritually formed person does not exist. A tree has no
choice about the kind of fruit it will produce, but humans do. We
produce either the fruit of Satan "the prince of this world, the
spirit of this age" or the new life through Christ and the Holy
Spirit. At some point in life everyone must answer the question:
"What power do you want forming you—Satan, self-reliance
and human wisdom, or God?"

God is concerned about our spiritual formation. For those
who choose to be formed by God, the issue is: "How may I enter
more fully into God's design for my life?" For the Pentecostal the
question is: "How does the baptism of the Spirit open the door
to empowerment and formation into the image of Christ?" Since
the character and ministry of Jesus are given to the Church, and

since the Spirit is given to believers through the baptism in the Holy Spirit, what then are we to proclaim and teach?

What is spiritual formation?

- Journey toward wholeness.
- Growth in the grace and knowledge of Christ.
- The process by which Christ's image is formed in us.
- Maturity through prayer, worship, relationships, and service.

The purpose of this book is to help you discover, explore, and appropriate the spiritual formation God offers you through faith development, prayer, Christian growth, and service. This will lead you to a fuller expression of Christ in your life and ministry, helping you experience and enjoy the presence and guidance of the Holy Spirit in your Christian journey.

MAN'S DILEMMA—A SEARCHING HEART

People struggle with the reality of God. The most frequently asked questions are, "Is there a God? Where is He? If God is real, how can I be sure He cares about me? Does He really love me?" When God is experienced, He reveals himself and fills the vacuum in each person's spiritual life. Personally experiencing God's truth and reality means understanding will never return to its former state. Adam and Eve were the first to learn this. They learned exactly what nakedness was as a result of disobedience. Their new spiritual experience left its mark—sin and death for all of us.

We know God and experience spiritual transformation by choosing to act on the truth revealed in the Bible. This personal experience is the connection between our spirit and our spiritual development. The simple, yet important question is, "Who and what are you allowing to influence the development of your spiritual life?" You have three choices: Satan, yourself, or God. Only one source leads to fulfillment—God.

THE FRONT LINE ISSUE

What energizes us in the realm of spiritual formation? What shapes and influences the spirit within us? World-class sporting events are a big influence in society, as are social, educational, political, religious, and entertainment activities. Each area has the potential to affect our lives for spiritual good or evil. Man's empathizing with victims of disaster, disease, and human violence shows a latent potential for good in the human spirit.

An individual's private world also contains negative life-shaping spiritual energies at work like revenge, overindulgence, promiscuity, mental and emotional struggles, and escapism. Why? Our spirit is restless, seeking relief from unfulfillment and pressures of life. God's Word explains why this is so.

The apostle Paul helped the Ephesian church analyze the spiritual dynamics in their lives. He said their former life of transgression and sin was influenced and energized by

> This world and...the ruler of the kingdom of the air, the spirit who is now at work in those who are disobedient. All of us also lived among them at one time, gratifying the cravings of our sinful nature and following its desires and thoughts (Ephesians 2:2, 3).

Paul knew this personally. It had been the controlling influence of his own spirit. Then Paul was transformed through an encounter with Jesus on the road to Damascus (Acts 9).

In his letter to the church at Rome, Paul described the realities of worldly spiritual formation. The spiritual forces of godlessness and wickedness were working to suppress the truth since "what may be known about God is plain to them" (Romans 1:18, 19). Herein lies the issue: a spiritual formational war is raging and no one is exempt from the battle. We are caught in the crossfire between God and Satan, and self and God. The battle for control transpires in our body, soul, mind, and relationships. God, our maker, is trying to reclaim us for himself. Returning our life to Him, letting Him be the ruler of our body, soul, and spirit instead of self or Satan, is the only way to put an end to this war.

The spirit within the human spirit expresses itself in many areas of life. Singers and writers express their feelings and thoughts through music and literature. Expressing the spirit within poses no problem. Humanity's problem is a sinful and depraved nature that prevents progress toward Christlikeness. The question then, in this winner-take-all battle, is: "Who will deliver us from this conflict?" This battle is resolved by learning how to receive the spirit God placed within Adam and Eve before they disobeyed and sinned.

THE GOSPEL IS FORMATIONAL

The power of Christian spiritual formation is what the gospel of Jesus Christ is all about. Divine love and grace penetrate the spiritual darkness that binds people to this evil world. How can God succeed in the face of these spirit-controlling environmental realities? He can because He wills to do so. God is not threatened by the forms of spiritual trickery, seduction, hedonism, or the moral, ethical, political, or educational bankruptcy that controls lives today. What is important for us to know is that God wants to engage us for a greater purpose than just knowing He exists.

Our humanity is settled at birth, but not our character. Once conception and gestation have occurred, a woman still faces labor and delivery. When the baby is born, "she has 'finished,' so to speak, her labor of creation and can enter into her 'rest.' But this is not a period of inactivity! Now the process of formation begins and continues."[2] God's plan is specifically aimed at our being like Jesus, even as the process of Christian spiritual formation begins (Romans 8:29). Our part in the process requires choosing daily whether or not we will live in obedience to God and walk in step with the Spirit (Galatians 5:25). Our obedience, daily commitment, and flexible Christlike attitude establish the requirements to know and fulfill God's plan in us and for us (Jeremiah 29:11, 12).

The King's Library

THEOLOGY AND THE FORMATIONAL PROCESS

Theologically—The apostle Paul said the aim of the Christian life is nothing less than a new creature perfect in Christ (Colossians 1:28), "created to be like God in true righteousness and holiness" (Ephesians 4:24), and renewed according to the "image of him who created him" (Colossians 3:10).

Paul develops the concept of Christian formation by using various theological images. He indicates that our life is hid with Christ in God when we choose to die to self and receive Christ into our lives (Colossians 3:3). In choosing death to self, we die with Christ and we identify with Him in His burial. The final dimension of the picture is developed in terms of our being raised with Christ through faith in the working of God. It is then that our spiritual life is spiritually and relationally linked to Christ as our living Savior and Lord (Colossians 2:12, 13; 3:1).

The Christian spiritual formation process begins with our relationship "in Christ." Pictorially, Paul uses the term "in Christ" to describe how the development of our spiritual character into Christlikeness is initiated.

Formationally—Christians who are gifted by the Holy Spirit are to teach and model how "not to conform" any longer to the pattern of this world, but be transformed by the renewing of one's mind in Christ. Paul was committed to helping individuals and churches connect with this "new life" given to those who daily give the rulership of their lives over to Jesus Christ. This was the theme of his ministry. Paul's goal was to motivate, teach, model, and help others be shaped into the "in Christ" character, mind, attitude, and life-style he was experiencing (1 Corinthians 11:1; 4:15–17; Romans 12:2–8, and Philippians 2:5).

Paul spoke lovingly and motivationally to Timothy about being a godly, effective servant for Christ. Paul referred to his own teaching, way of life, purpose, faith, patience, love, endurance, persecution, and suffering as a resource for Timothy in the development of his Christian life and ministry. Paul expected

Timothy, as a faithful, proven minister of the gospel, to guard the good formational training he had received from himself and the Holy Spirit (1 Timothy 6:20; 2 Timothy 1:14; 4:5). In other words, Paul was pumped up about being a "balcony person" in the Pentecostal spiritual formation and development of Timothy. Here is the bottom line of Christian pastoral and lay ministry—developing homegrown leaders for ministry in the local church.

LEAVING ROOM FOR RENEWAL

Thomas Merton wrote: "It's not complicated to lead the spiritual life but it is difficult."[3] The future of the Church and Christian ministry and our formation in Christ is closely associated with our willingness to say, "Yes, Lord, yes." To initiate Christ's formation and renewal in your life today, you must begin by saying yes to the Lord's will and His way, by trusting and obeying Scripture, and by agreeing with the Holy Spirit with your whole heart.

God wants to personally encounter you for two reasons. First, He wants you to experience the transforming power of Jesus in your life. As Peters and Waterman have said:

> Every excellent company is clear on what it stands for, and takes the process of value shaping seriously.[4]

God wants you to know Christ, who is life eternal (John 17:3). Paul valued this above all other knowledge—to know Christ and Him crucified. Jesus is the only source of wholeness we have to give the world and each other. Our theology and work for the Lord is based on this plain truth: Christ

> gave himself for our sins to rescue us from the present evil age, according to the will of our God and Father (Galatians 1:4).

When we disciple another person to the lordship of Jesus, we are actualizing our own worship of Him as Lord.

Secondly, God wants you to experience the baptism of the Holy Spirit so you can perpetuate the spiritual formation ministry of Jesus as Savior, healer, baptizer, and coming King.

THE IMPORTANCE OF YOUR JOURNEY

Why is a clear understanding of your formational journey important? First, it is important to respond positively and take advantage of the foundations which God has laid in your life. You are not the product of a factory production line. God has been providentially working through your birth, family, environment, and historical events. As J. Robert Clinton rightly states: "You might find this hard to believe that God was working through your family or your environment, especially if these were not godly influences, but He was."[5] Your experiences enable you to help others respond positively to the foundations in their lives. You will be motivated to lay a good foundation in the lives of others—a foundation upon which God can develop healthy, hearty, vibrant servants for Jesus, whether they be children, youth, or adults who are new to the things of God.

Second, it is beneficial to see and value all that must go into the development of a healthy Christian. As you pray and learn to hear God, as you face tests that develop your character, and as you grow in understanding, discernment, and obedience, then and only then will you be better equipped to assist others in their formation. Clinton has noted:

> The amazing thing is that…God is primarily working in the leader (not through him or her). Though there may be fruitfulness in ministry, the major work is that which God is doing to and in the leader, not through him or her. Most emerging leaders don't recognize this. They evaluate productivity, activities, fruitfulness, etc. But God is quietly, often in unusual ways, trying to get the leader to see that one ministers out of what one is. God is concerned with what we are. We want to learn a thousand things because there is so much to learn and do. But He will teach us one thing, perhaps in a thousand ways: "I am forming Christ in you." It is this that will give power to your ministry.[6]

You should find yourself anticipating, with excitement, that God is forming and empowering you through the Spirit so He can use you to form others in the image of Christ.

Adapting this theological picture to your life will lead you to a more meaningful ministry with God. "Effective leaders," says J. Robert Clinton, "increasingly perceive their ministries in terms of a lifetime perspective…. If you know that God will be developing you over a lifetime, you'll most likely stay for the whole ride."[7] These are things which relate to the ministry you have or will have. There is a correlation between your journey and those who are receiving instruction for their journey from you. Reflecting and responding to critical incidents in your life where God taught you and shaped your spirit is central to your spiritual formation and to your helping others in their journey.

As Christians, Jesus sets our ministry formation agenda. He taught with love, wisdom, patience, and authority. He also taught with a sense of destiny and a sense of leisure. Our responsibility is to do likewise.

Doing the ministry of Jesus requires individual learning. Learning to minister will include pain, prayer, struggle, and faith. It will be two-dimensional: First, genuine ministry comes from God. You must know Him to minister effectively since all ministry is His ministry and He doesn't give His ministry to someone He doesn't know. Secondly, genuine ministry is horizontal—it's relational. You can count on the horizontal/relational issues staying with you through every phase of life and ministry. Relationships provide ministry challenge, accountability, and personal growth.

We are commissioned to make disciples who can make disciples—disciples who can minister according to the Spirit's power, gifts, and calling upon their lives. We must focus on helping boys and girls, teens, and adults be formed "in Christ" so the Church will be vibrant and authentic. Christianity can become a religious system of belief, buildings, and budgets. If you and those you disciple are a godly spiritual formation force in this world, then the Church will truly be able to encourage people to offer God their sin, self, and life.

FORMING PEOPLE FOR MINISTRY

Developing homegrown leaders is fundamental to being the Church—the body of Christ. Since Pentecost marks the beginning of the Church, there is a lesson associated with its beginning that is foundational to its future. Holy Spirit baptism will produce more than tongues-speaking Christians. It will produce praying, witnessing, teaching, preaching, healing, hope-giving, faith-filled disciples of Christ who will transmit the gospel throughout their city and the world. The formation of these leaders, however, begins with Christ flowing into your life and ends with Christ and you flowing into the lives of both Christians and non-Christians. God uses your experience in Scripture, worship, prayer, and in Holy Spirit baptism to influence others. Unless your interior life and exterior ministry overflow with the life of Christ, you have no way of truly helping someone acquire Christian spiritual formation.

Churches should not only make their individual members aware of all the opportunities for and the benefits of spiritual growth, they should also equip them for service to others. Unless Christians are challenged to minister for the Lord, God's plan of reconciliation cannot reach those without Christ. People will die if their spirits are formed by their own self-reliance or by the worldly formation found in Satan's snare. Paul says God has given the ministry of reconciliation to all of us who are new creatures in Christ (2 Corinthians 5:18–20). It's one thing to be a new creature in Christ and another to be bold and passionate about spreading the liberating Word. We need empowerment from the Holy Spirit to proclaim the claims of the gospel to the people of this present age.

It is the Pentecostal encounter with Jesus that personalizes the matter of spiritual growth and Christian spiritual formation. Not only will the Church be severely weakened if it does not identify, equip, and deploy people in ministry according to the gifts given them by the Holy Spirit (1 Peter 4:10), but also it will be weakened if it does not perpetuate the Pentecostal experience. The normative source for ministry empowerment is Spirit baptism, which motivates workers to accomplish the evangelism and discipleship goal God mandates. It is the formation that comes from the baptism in the Holy Spirit that empowers the ministry of Jesus in word and deed in the believer, in the world, and in the Church. Speaking in tongues, which accompanies Spirit baptism, is also linked to personal, ongoing transformation and empowerment in the Christian's life and service (1 Corinthians 14:3).

PENTECOSTAL CHRISTIAN SPIRITUAL FORMATION

Pentecostal Christian spiritual formation is no less a formational experience than the new birth. It is essential to the Church and every believer whom God has commissioned to serve the Lord until He comes again. One might argue that herein is a key to the threshold of Christianity. Will those whose ministry is preaching, teaching, discipling, and equipping people to minister for Christ be motivated to boldly and tenaciously seek the Holy Spirit for the power to sustain and fulfill Christ's ministry today?

The authentic empowerment for life and ministry can only come when we embrace the power which God birthed into the Church by the Holy Spirit at Pentecost. You can point to no other dynamic in the Bible that so profoundly speaks of the way God makes Christ real. Through the baptism in and the gifts of the Holy Spirit, God expresses himself continually in believers and the Church.

Our progress in spiritual formation depends on God and ourselves—God's grace and our own will to be fully formed in Christ. We must have a real living determination if we are to experience all that the living Christ would form of himself in our lives. What other direction is there for us? None, but the place of prayer and humble openness to Christ and God's agent of spiritual formation—the Holy Spirit.

2

The Development Dynamic

by Rob Burkhart

Every living thing grows. At least, they are designed to grow. Growth and development are an integral part of God's design of our world and reality. The pattern is all around us: conception, birth, growth, maturity, and reproduction. What is true in the physical is equally true in the spiritual. The new birth ought to be followed by a period of growth and development that leads to maturity and reproduction.

But healthy development isn't automatic. Tragically, some know the agony of healthy and mature minds trapped in handicapped bodies. Others are forever children in adult bodies. Some fail to achieve emotional, social, or moral maturity. Like an unfinished paint by numbers picture, the pattern is clear, but the colors are missing.

Many experience the joy of the new birth but fail to achieve spiritual maturity. They seem forever trapped on a single spiritual plateau and are unwilling or unable to grow. Spiritual immaturity has far greater and more serious consequences for the person and for those they influence.

DIMENSIONS OF HUMAN DEVELOPMENT

Throughout their lives people have the potential to develop in six distinct areas:

- physically
- intellectually
- emotionally
- socially
- morally
- spiritually.

The first and most predictable area is the physical. Physical development provides the bedrock of our understanding of human development in all other areas, including the spiritual.

People also develop intellectually. Jean Piaget, in his book *The Psychology of Intelligence*, described four stages of intellectual development: from the infant's reflexes (the *sensor-motor* stage), to the pre-logical thinking and fantasy of childhood (the *pre-operational* stage), to the *concrete operations* stage, and ultimately to adult abstract thinking (the *formal operations* stage).

Benjamin Bloom looked at intellectual development differently in *Handbook of Educational Objectives: Cognitive Domain* and developed these: *knowledge, comprehension, application, analysis, synthesis,* and *evaluation*. Malcolm Knowles, on the other hand, in *The Modern Practice of Adult Education*, compared *andragogy,* the way adults learn, to *pedagogy*, the way children learn.

Third, people develop emotionally. Abraham Maslow, in *Motivation and Personality*, identified stages of need that are closely tied to emotional development. He arranged these needs in a hierarchy and asserted that lower needs must be gratified if the person is to meet higher needs.

In *Childhood and Society,* Erik Erikson identified a list of qualities that emerge from critical periods of development. These qualities show the strength of the individual in relation to social institutions.

Daniel Levinson, in *Seasons of a Man's Life*, identified developmental periods in early and middle adulthood with the major related tasks. His research was based in social psychology and was strongly influenced by Erikson. Building on Levinson, Gail Sheehy wrote *Passages: Predictable Crises of Adult Life,* which focuses on the emotional and social development of men and women throughout adult life.

Lawrence Kohlberg identified six stages of moral development. These stages define the flow of the development of moral reasoning. His work shows that moral reasoning develops from *concrete-physical concerns* with reference to *self*, then with reference to *external authority*, and finally progressing to an *internal commitment to ethical principles*.

James Fowler attempted to apply developmental principles to faith development. He asserts six stages ranging from *primal faith* to *universalizing faith*.

DEVELOPMENTAL ASSUMPTIONS

A developmental understanding of life is based on ten important assumptions.

1. Despite a wide range of differences, people are more alike than different.

2. This essential of humanity shared by all people is inherent.

3. The patterns of development are in the very nature of mankind; that is, people share developmental patterns even if they don't share the same environment or experiences.

4. These growth patterns cannot be significantly altered.

5. Development occurs in several areas of growth—physical, mental, emotional, social, moral, and spiritual.

6. Development must be understood holistically. The various aspects of growth and development are related to each other.

7. The individual's environment tends to facilitate or inhibit development.

8. While development involves acquiring abilities, it is primarily a matter of losing limitations.

9. Development in any given area can be stalemated by adverse conditions.

10. Fulfilling the continuing pattern of development throughout one's life is essential to fulfilling our humanity.

THE BIBLE AND SPIRITUAL GROWTH

Pentecostal Christian Spiritual Formation Is God's Will For Each Believer

"Epaphras, who is one of you, a servant of Christ, saluteth you, always laboring fervently for you in prayers, that ye may stand perfect and complete in all the will of God" (Colossians 4:12). Unfortunately, many believers see fulfilling God's will in terms of external obedience rather than internal development. God intends that His children grow up. Perpetual spiritual immaturity is both a tragedy and an affront to Christ's sacrifice.

Attaining Spiritual Maturity Is A Developmental Process

"Brothers, I could not address you as spiritual but as worldly— mere infants in Christ. I gave you milk, not solid food, for you were not ready for it. Indeed, you are still not ready" (1 Corinthians 3:1, 2). "When I was a child, I talked like a child, I thought like a child, I reasoned like a child. When I became a man, I put childish ways behind me" (1 Corinthians 13:11).

Note several things in Paul's analogy. First, believers do not attain instant maturity as part of salvation or the baptism in the Holy Spirit. Second, spiritual development is progressive. After a time at one level, believers should be ready to move on to the next. Finally, while development occurs in a particular pattern, it doesn't happen at a predictable rate. Paul expected the believers at Corinth to be further along than they were.

Spiritual Development Can Be Stalemated

"In fact, though by this time you ought to be teachers, you need someone to teach you the elementary truths of God's word all over again. You need milk, not solid food!" (Hebrews 5:12). Clearly the author of Hebrews viewed his readers as cases of arrested development. They should have progressed beyond the *elementary truths*, but hadn't. Spiritual formation isn't instantaneous, and it isn't automatic. There is no guarantee of the rate of development or even that the believer will ultimately become spiritually mature. Finally, both internal and external factors impact spiritual development.

Mastery Of One Level Of Development Is A Prerequisite For The Next Stage

"You need someone to teach you the elementary truths of God's word all over again" (Hebrews 5:12). "Therefore let us leave the elementary teachings about Christ and go on to maturity, not laying again the foundation" (Hebrews 6:1). These believers had failed to master the *elementary truths* and could not move on in maturity. Their failure to outgrow this spiritual *milk* prevented them from being "acquainted with the teaching about righteousness" (Hebrews 5:13). Failure to master the lessons of one stage dooms the believer to going over the same ground again and again until mastery is achieved.

Pentecostal Christian Spiritual Development Demands Personal Effort

"Solid food is for the mature, who by constant use have trained themselves to distinguish good from evil" (Hebrews 5:14). "Not that I have already obtained all this, or have already been made perfect....But one thing I do: Forgetting what is behind and straining toward what is ahead, I press on toward the goal to win the prize for which God has called me heavenward in Christ Jesus" (Philippians 3:12–14). Believers are responsible for "training themselves." Spiritual development requires the same intense effort as an athlete training for competition. Spiritual development requires a personal vision, motivation, and determination to go on with God.

THE NATURE OF SPIRITUAL GROWTH

In Ephesians 4:11–16, Paul summarizes the results, lists key elements, and outlines the process of spiritual growth. Notice Paul's definition of maturity: "Attaining to the whole measure of the fullness of Christ" (Ephesians 4:13). This phrase refers to the fullness that belongs to Christ; the sum of the qualities which make Him who He is. Only when these qualities are an integral part of the believer's very nature can it be said that he has reached maturity and attained the goal set before him.

THE RESULTS OF SPIRITUAL GROWTH

Paul also defines the results of achieving this maturity. First, believers leave the instability and vulnerability of spiritual infancy. It is spiritual maturity that protects the believer from the onslaught of godless men and ideas.

Second, mature believers find their place in the body of Christ in accordance with their Spirit-given gifts. The mature believer is best able to contribute his unique gifts and abilities to the healthy function of the Body.

Unity is the third significant result of spiritual maturity. Elsewhere (1 Corinthians 3:1–4) Paul pointed to disunity as evidenced by jealousy and quarreling as proof of spiritual immaturity and worldliness. In Ephesians 4:16, Paul points to unity as the positive outcome of spiritual maturity.

The body of Christ is built up as a result of individual spiritual maturity. It is built up in strength as well as in size. As individuals mature, they add their strength of commitment and character to the Body. New people are reached with the gospel as they see believers living up to their high calling.

Finally, each level of spiritual maturity introduces new levels to which one may aspire. Once a believer stands on the heights of a given level of spiritual growth, he encounters new vistas. In a real sense the reward and result of achieving a degree of spiritual maturity is another level for which to strive.

KEY ELEMENTS OF SPIRITUAL GROWTH

Prior to examining the elements of growth, Paul described several important ideas that should be noted. First, the potential for spiritual growth is inherent in the life of every believer. It is the inevitable result of the new birth.

Second, while the pattern of growth is universal, the pace of growth is unique. Different people experience different stages at their own pace and in their own way. While the presence of these elements enhance and their absence encumbers spiritual growth, they neither cause nor shape it.

Lastly, the individual believer's readiness to move to the next stage is critical. Each element plays a significant role at each stage of spiritual growth. However, the form each element takes and the mix of elements is different at each level. Meaningless experiences at one level become vital at another.

Knowledge

Twice in this passage Paul referred to knowledge. He related the knowledge of the Son of God and becoming mature (Ephesians 4:13) and taught that "speaking the truth in love, we will in all things grow up into him who is the Head, that is, Christ" (Ephesians 4:15). There is no doubt that what the believer knows and understands is critical to healthy Pentecostal Christian spiritual formation.

Available to the believer are several sources of biblical and spiritual knowledge. First, the believer can hear the spoken word. Apostles, prophets, evangelists, pastors, and teachers are given to the Church "to prepare God's people." The wisdom, guidance, instruction, and insights of church leadership can contribute much to a receptive believer's spiritual growth.

Spiritual understanding can also be gleaned from the experiences and insights of other believers. Through their writings, spiritual giants of the past are available to today's growing Christian. Others more spiritually mature are available as friends and mentors. This type of informal instruction is part of God's plan. "Likewise, teach the older women to be reverent in the way they live....Then they can train the younger women...so that no one will malign the word of God" (Titus 2:3–5).

A second source of knowledge is the written word. Spiritual maturity just isn't attainable without daily, consistent, disciplined study. Unfortunately, many believers lack the discipline or desire for such study. The absence of this essential spiritual food leads to malnourished souls and spiritual anemia. Finally, Pentecostal believers know the joy of the Holy Spirit's ministry. "God has revealed it to us by his Spirit.... No one knows the thoughts of God except the Spirit of God...that we may understand what God has freely given us" (1 Corinthians 2:10–12).

The internal voice of the Spirit and the manifestations of the gifts of the Spirit in the Body are powerful sources of spiritual knowledge and understanding. However, the fear of error has led many, even in Pentecostal circles, to shy away from this important source of spiritual understanding. But God has given safeguards. First, the internal voice of the Spirit is always consistent with the external voice of the Bible. Second, the believer can rely on the confirmation of others in the church.

Spiritual development is clearly linked to intellectual development. No one expects a child to grasp spiritual truth in the same way as an adult. These limitations, however, do not mean that children cannot experience spiritual growth. It only means that a child's spiritual understanding develops within the parameters of his intellectual development.

There are implications for the Bible teacher. First, biblical knowledge is critical for healthy spiritual development. Second, all learners, regardless of age or intellect, benefit from the study of God's Word. The fact different learners grasp biblical truth at different levels doesn't diminish its significance. The ministry of teaching is a high calling, essential for healthy believers and churches and thus deserves the teacher's very best.

Emotion

Spiritual development is linked to our emotional response to God and His people. It is truth spoken in love (Ephesians 4:15) that results in spiritual growth. And it is in love that the Body grows and is built up (Ephesians 4:16). Without biblical love, biblical knowledge will not enhance spiritual development.

In Ephesians, Paul saw this love functioning in two dimensions. First, spiritual truth was to be communicated in a loving atmosphere. Love is both the controlling factor and the emotional litmus test of a biblical teaching ministry. If teachers truly love their students, they will be concerned with insuring a whole range of positive emotional experiences. They will be just as concerned in eliminating a whole range of others.

Second, love is the guiding principle of Christian action. The Body "builds itself up in love, as each part does its work" (Ephesians 4:16). Love of God and others becomes the primary motivating force for Christian service.

Love is not just the basic requirement for biblical teaching and service. Love is what people should feel. Surrounding love is a constellation of emotions that ought to pervade the believer's life and experience. "The fruit of the Spirit is love, joy, peace, patience, kindness, goodness, faithfulness, gentleness and self-control. Against such things there is no law" (Galatians 5:22,23).

Elsewhere love is pictured not as the center of an emotional constellation, but as the end of a developmental process.

> For this very reason, make every effort to add to your faith goodness; and to goodness, knowledge; and to knowledge, self-control; and to self-control, perseverance; and to perseverance, godliness; and to godliness, brotherly kindness; and to brotherly kindness, love. For if you possess these qualities in increasing measure, they will keep you from being ineffective and unproductive in your knowledge of our Lord Jesus Christ (2 Peter 1:5–8).

Note several things in Peter's description of emotional and spiritual development. First, it is a process. The believer *adds* qualities to his life. Second, this pattern of development that requires mastery of one quality before another can be added. The believer must put forth effort to insure proper development. Lastly, knowledge and emotional development are linked.

Healthy spiritual development is linked with healthy emotional development. Children feel differently than adults, and adults experience emotions differently than adolescents. These differences do not mean that spiritual development cannot occur—only that it occurs within the parameters of that individual's emotional development.

The significant role of emotion in spiritual development has several implications for the Bible teacher. Not only must the teacher prepare not only the intellectual environment, but also the emotional environment. Also, the teacher must be sensitive to the emotional state of his students and respond accordingly. And finally, the teacher needs to relate biblical content to the learner's emotional reality.

Relationships

Pentecostal Christian spiritual formation is a relational process. The monks and hermits of early Christendom were wrong. True spiritual development cannot take place in solitude. It only happens in context of the body of Christ. Paul stressed the importance of the Body in Ephesians 4:11–16.

First, God gave gifted people (apostles, prophets, evangelists, pastors and teachers) to equip believers. Second, the believer is pictured as an integral part of the Body who contributes to the other members and to the health and unity of the Body.

There are five different levels of human relationships. *Strangers* are those who we know little or nothing about. An *acquaintance* is someone we know something about. *Friends* are those whom we know well and care for. *Family* is not limited to those who are related, but exhibits greater levels of commitment and belonging than found among friends. The fifth level, more *intimate* than friend or family, is sometimes called *lover*.

These levels can be thought of in different ways. First, they can be viewed in terms of commitment. Strangers demand little or no commitment, while family and lovers require total commitment. Another way to look at these relationships is in terms of the number of people one can relate to at each level. That number decreases as the level of commitment increases.

Christ relates to His followers as friends, family, and lovers —not as strangers and acquaintances. "You are my friends if you do what I command. I no longer call you servants, because a servant does not know his master's business. Instead, I have called you friends" (John 15:14,15). "If we are children, then we are heirs—heirs of God and co-heirs with Christ" (Romans 8:17). "As my Father has loved me, so have I loved you. Now remain in my love" (John 15:9).

Developing quality relationships within the body of Christ is an integral part of spiritual development. Without those relationships, the believer is divorced from a primary source of growth, guidance, and love. Learning to love as Christ loves demands that the believer jettison much of what the world teaches. Jealousy, competition, conquest, and dominance fade in the face of love, cooperation, submission, and service.

The kind of relationships believers develop is linked to their social development. At different developmental stages people develop different relationships with their peers, parents, siblings, teachers, and others. But at every stage people need healthy, loving relationships.

The Bible teacher has a vital role in this process. First, the teacher should model loving relationships by refusing to let any learner be just a stranger or acquaintance. Next, the teacher should help his class become a *family*. Encouraging interaction, working together in class, organizing projects, and providing opportunities to have fun together are ways to accomplish this.

Behavior

Believers are being prepared for their "works of service" (Ephesians 4:12). The Body builds itself up in love "as each part does its work" (Ephesians 4:16). Christian action is both the result of spiritual maturity and the process by which believers grow and develop.

There is an ongoing dynamic interaction between biblical action and the other elements of spiritual development. "Do not merely listen to the word, and so deceive yourselves. Do what it says" (James 1:22). "In the same way, faith by itself, if it is not accompanied by action, is dead" (James 2:17). "Not everyone who says to me, 'Lord, Lord,' will enter the kingdom of heaven, but only he who does the will of my Father who is in heaven" (Matthew 7:21). Biblical knowledge without Christian action violates God's plan for spiritual development. But behavior linked with knowledge creates opportunities for spiritual growth.

Christian action demands much of the believer. It requires an application of biblical knowledge. By its very nature it most often happens in relationship with others. These acts are emotionally charged. Finally, Christian actions create the need and opportunities for prayer and other spiritual disciplines.

Not every act performed by a Christian is a Christian act. It is only when the believer imitates Christ in both attitude and act that his actions are truly Christian.

"Jesus Christ, who gave himself for us to redeem us from all wickedness and to purify for himself a people that are his very own, eager to do what is good" (Titus 2:13,14). In these verses Paul described Christ's work and set the standard for truly Christian behavior. First, such acts are self-sacrificing, not self-serving. Much church activity, done under the guise of Christian action, is of the church, by the church, and for the church. It never calls for selfless sacrifice. Second, Christ gave himself to "redeem us from all wickedness" (Titus 2:14). The primary purpose of Christian action ought to be the redemption of lost people. Much of what is considered today as Christian action is noble and important, but has no connection to reaching the lost and so fails to truly imitate Christ.

Christ also gave himself to purify for himself a people. Acts that develop personal holiness are critical to fulfilling Christ's call. But the believer must also work for a just and holy society. Working for those things is just as important as working against things that pollute society.

Christ also came to create a people that are His very own. Building unity and harmony in the body of Christ is a fourth criteria of Christian action. All too often issues of style and self-aggrandizement and social norms have splintered the church. Actions that foster love and unity between believers and churches are critical to Pentecostal Christian spiritual formation.

Finally, Christ sought to create a people eager to do what is good. Truly Christian acts are carried out with an attitude of joy and eagerness. If done begrudgingly or under duress, believers lose the benefit. The attitude is as important as the act.

Clearly, Christian action is linked to physical, intellectual, and emotional development. Young children simply are not capable of the same actions as their parents or older siblings.

But all believers are capable of acting on biblical truth in appropriate and beneficial ways. The missing ingredient is often a creative Bible teacher who can guide his learners to action.

There are several very important implications for the Bible teacher. First, every classroom should become a laboratory for Christian action. The teacher should take the truths taught in Scripture and look for ways the class can act on them in a truly Christian way. Second, believers need the opportunity to discuss and reflect on their experiences. This process is another way to link biblical truth with the believer's life. The teacher must also help learners focus on the motivation and attitude behind their behavior.

Spirituality

The final element in Pentecostal Christian spiritual formation is spirituality. A believer's walk with Christ is at once the foundation and the fountain of spiritual development.

The classical spiritual disciplines of prayer, study, meditation, and fasting are essential. However, they have largely fallen into disuse. Many believers fail to see their importance. Others feel that they do not have the time or are unwilling to make the effort.

One point should be made clear: Spiritual growth is the work of the Holy Spirit, not the result of human effort. Followers of other religions are much more diligent in their religious practices than many Christians. But their efforts are futile. It is the Spirit that causes real growth in the life of the believer.

What, then, is the place of spiritual disciplines in the life of the believer? These disciplines open the believer to the work of the Spirit. It is in prayer, fasting, study, and meditation that the voice of the Spirit can be heard, the hand of the Spirit can work, and the presence of the Spirit can be felt.

The Bible teacher can do much to help his learners develop a vital, living walk with Christ. First, the teacher can stress the importance of walking with Christ. Teachers can also model these spiritual disciplines for their classes and demonstrate how to incorporate them into daily life. Making prayer, study, and meditation a part of the class experience and encouraging fasting is another way teachers can help learners employ these disciplines.

Finally, teachers must develop their own vital walk with Christ. Spirituality is not an academic subject. It is life with Christ. It does little good to teach spiritual disciplines apart from the vitality of true spiritual life. Learners who sense Jesus in their teacher will be drawn to greater heights of spirituality. Learners who sense that their teacher's faith is only an empty shell will be driven from Christ and His Church.

THE END OF THE MATTER

In the final analysis, Pentecostal Christian spiritual formation isn't about what the believer does. It's about what God does in the life of the believer. But the believer's understanding of spiritual truth, his relationships, his life-style, his walk with Christ, and his attitude toward Him all enhance or inhibit that work. Pentecostal Christian spiritual formation is man cooperating with God's plan, following God's will, and submitting to God's way.

3

Methods
For
Teaching Prayer

by Rob Blakney

A man stranded in the desert frantically searches for water. He puts all of his energy into finding water. He knows without it he will perish. It is necessary, essential for life. Nothing will serve as its substitute. A Christian living in today's world is also involved in an intense search—a search for the answer to how he can stay alive in Christ. The answer is simple: He must have prayer to survive. Without it, he, too, will probably perish. It is necessary. Nothing can serve as its substitute. It is as fundamental to the Christian as water is to the human body.

REEMPHASIZE PRAYER

Prayer, probably because of its frequent mention in the Bible, is often taken for granted. Young's *Analytical Concordance to the Bible* lists *pray* 201 times with 18 different meanings. It also lists the word *prayer* 133 times with 11 different meanings. This does not include many other words that refer to "pray" or "prayer." Since prayer is such a common Bible teaching and is such a foundation to the Christian faith, it must be stressed and reemphasized regularly to both new and mature Christians. If the disciples—men who walked with Jesus—needed to be taught how to pray, how much more should our students be taught to pray.

TEACHING PRAYER WEEKLY

Probably, for most teachers, the curriculum they use emphasizes prayer only once or twice per year. Is it possible to teach about prayer on a weekly basis and yet not cause prayer "burnout" by the students? Is it possible to regularly stress prayer without shunning or diluting the many other important teachings in God's Word? The answer is "Yes," if it is done creatively and with passion. Several suggestions that require less than 5 minutes per week are listed below.

THIRTY-SECOND MINI-TEACHINGS

Every lesson should begin with prayer, not only for the understanding of the lesson content but also for the needs of the students. When the teacher demonstrates his/her concern for the student through asking for personal prayer needs, the student is more likely to listen to one who cares. However, before personal requests are given, why not teach the students with a 30-second "mini-burst" on prayer using one of the several hundred verses referring to prayer? Listed below are 26 mini-teachings, including the verse or verse portion (KJV) and a simple, teaching statement.

1. James 5:16. "The effectual fervent prayer of a righteous man availeth much." We must try harder to live holy lives if we want our prayers to be answered.

2. Matthew 6:9. God is "Our Father which art in heaven." God can more clearly see the whole picture from heaven and therefore can answer our prayers perfectly.

3. Psalm 66:18. "If I regard iniquity in my heart, the Lord will not hear me." Therefore, we must search our hearts before we pray.

4. Hebrews 4:16. "Come boldly unto the throne of grace." We are given permission to come before our Heavenly Father.

5. Matthew 6:10. "Thy will be done." Therefore, after we pray we still yield to His will and His answer.

6. Matthew 6:11. "Give us this day our daily bread." It is not selfish to pray for our daily material needs.

7. Isaiah 56:7. "Mine house shall be called a house of prayer." Prayer should be a regular part of our times at God's house and during the Sunday school hour.

8. Romans 8:26. When we know not what we should pray for, then the Spirit will make "intercession for us with groanings which cannot be uttered." Sometimes, only the Holy Spirit within us knows how to pray.

9. Revelation 5:8. "Golden vials full of odors, which are the prayers of saints." Our prayers are considered precious in heaven.

10. Matthew 26:41. "Watch and pray, that ye enter not into temptation." Prayer can help us stay out of temptation's way.

11. First Thessalonians 5:17. "Pray without ceasing." Prayer should be a part of every activity of the day.

12. John 15:7. "If ye abide in me, and my words abide in you, ye shall ask what ye will, and it shall be done unto you." Prayer is answered as we keep God's Word. Read your Bible daily.

13. Matthew 18:19. "If two of you shall agree on earth as touching any thing that they shall ask, it shall be done for them of my Father which is in heaven." It is good to have a prayer partner, attend prayer meetings, and agree together in class for prayer needs.

14. Second Chronicles 7:14. If we humble ourselves, our prayers will be answered. We must constantly remember we are saved by grace, not by works.

15. First John 3:22. "Whatsoever we ask, we receive of him because we keep his commandments." We must live according to the Scriptures if we want our prayers answered.

16. Mark 1:35. "[Jesus] prayed." Therefore, we should imitate Him and pray also.

17. Psalm 102:17. "He will regard the prayer of the destitute." No matter our condition, God can hear our prayer.

18. Psalm 55:17. "Evening, and morning, and at noon, will I pray." We need to pray often.

19. Matthew 17:21. "This kind goeth not out but by prayer and fasting." Some things will happen only if we pray.

20. First Timothy 2:8. "I will therefore that men pray everywhere, lifting up holy hands, without wrath and doubting." We should pray without anger and without doubt in our lives.

21. James 5:17. "Elijah was a man just like us. He prayed earnestly" (NIV) and the Lord heard him. God will answer the prayer of common people just like us.

22. First Peter 3:7. "Husbands, ...giving honor unto the wife, ...that your prayers will be not hindered." Personal relationships should be pure in order for our prayers to be answered.

23. James 4:3. "Ye ask, and received not, because ye ask amiss, that ye may consume it upon your lusts." Pray for the right reasons, and not always for our own personal needs.

24. Second Corinthians 12:8,9. Paul sought the Lord three times and He said, "My grace is sufficient for thee." God will always hear our prayers and He will always answer them His special way, not necessarily our way.

25. Psalm 4:3. "Know that the Lord hath set apart him that is godly for himself: the Lord will hear when I call unto Him." The Lord takes notice and hears those who are godly.

26. Proverbs 15:29. The Lord hears "the prayer of the righteous." A "right-standing" with God assures answered prayers.

THIRTY-SECOND TESTIMONIES

Allowing students to share testimonies of how God answered their prayers accomplishes at least two things. First, it builds the faith of classmates before they pray. Secondly, it emphasizes that prayer is real, it works, and it is not a waste of time. To initiate these testimony times, the teacher should recruit one or two students a week prior to class and ask them to share a short testimony of answered prayer. Later, the teacher may want to appoint a prayer chairman to help coordinate testimonies.

WEEKLY PRAYER LOGS

By recording prayer requests of his students, the teacher makes a powerful statement to the students. The students understand that the teacher really cares and that they are not just "going through the motions" when they pray in class. If the list is reviewed weekly in class and answered prayers are checked off and new prayers "added," the class members' faith is increased and challenged. The students know they can come to the class with prayer needs and that they will be added to the list. The teacher can go a step further by contacting students throughout the week to check on their prayer needs.

PRAYER HOMEWORK

If possible, the teacher should make a list of the prayer needs and send the list home with the students. The list could be copied or duplicated by the individual that normally gathers the class records and then distributed before the class is dismissed. Will all of the students pray weekly for the needs on the list? Maybe not. However, we must challenge all to pray.

TEACHERS PRAYER LIFE—A TEACHING TOOL

If the student regularly hears his teacher refer to his own prayer life, the importance of prayer is again reinforced. The teacher should regularly allude to his answered, unanswered, and delayed prayers. This is an indirect way to teach about prayer and brings prayer from the abstract to the concrete as they hear how a real, living God does indeed respond to our requests. To tell of unanswered or delayed prayers is not being negative. Rather, it is showing the omniscience of God.

CLASS PRAYER PROJECTS

A unique and powerful way to teach about prayer is to plan a class prayer project. The project should be one that requires continual prayer but has possibilities of having prayer needs answered soon and new needs added. Some examples are: (1) Praying for missionaries, their needs, and their families. The class may want to adopt a particular member of the missionary's family. (2) Praying for specific ministries within the church. (3) Praying for the pastor, staff, and leadership of the church. (4) Praying for government leaders, issues, elections, etc.

In a society that has seemingly become more selfish, this type of intercessory prayer teaches the class the importance of praying for more than just personal needs.

DIFFERENT TYPES OF PRAYER

The most common type of classroom prayer time is the typical receiving of prayer requests followed by the teacher leading audibly in prayer. Sometimes the entire class will join together audibly in prayer. However, there are many other ways to lead the class in prayer that are lively, exciting, and personal. Some suggestions are listed below:

1. Have each student write his personal prayer. Collect the prayers, shuffle them, and give them back to the students. Have each person, if possible, read the prayer written by someone else.

2. Record the needs of the students on a chalkboard. Ask the students to glance at the board as they silently pray for each need. This allows each person to pray and not be intimidated by using his own personal style of praying.

3. Before or after praying for the class' requests, read a Bible prayer or praise.

4. After the requests have been made known to the class, ask the class to quietly meditate on the needs, asking the Lord how they can respond to the needs. Some may even share how they will help meet the need.

5. To help structure prayer time, read each of the requests and allow 10–15 seconds of prayer before reading the next need.

PRAYER TIME—FOCUSED AND PERSONAL

A very powerful way to keep the class prayer time focused is to take time once or twice a year to have the class list several names or attributes of God. Keep the list very visible in the classroom throughout the year. Four or five times a year ask all of your class members to condense their prayer needs to one sentence. Have them choose one of the names of God that has been listed and begin their one sentence prayer need with one of the names. Allow them to pray their prayers aloud. For example: "Healer, please touch my mother's arthritis," or "Provider, please provide for us a new refrigerator," or "Omniscient One, please give me wisdom concerning a new job opportunity." This is a powerful teaching method that focuses and personalizes the prayer time for all who attend.

PRAYER—A SUBTLE DE-EMPHASIS

No teacher would ever purposely de-emphasize prayer. However, some may do it inadvertently. Tips to avoid accidentally de-emphasizing prayer:

1. Pray about the lesson content and class needs before any dismissal bells ring. At the sound of the bell, often the students' minds and spirits go immediately into the transition time between class and worship service. Often the many distractions that take place after the bell rings make it difficult to pray seriously. One possibility is to have one, two, or three mini-prayer times throughout the lesson.

2. When the students sense the prayer led by the teacher is not "heart-felt," they pay less attention to the teacher and see prayer only as a part of the Christianity "game."

3. When a student requests prayer for a particular need and it is forgotten, the student is discouraged. Always record the prayer requests as they are received.

4. Prayer that is joked about or done in a frivolous way is harmful. Refreshments must be put down, talking must stop, and the teacher must lovingly take control of the prayer time.

5. Make sure that all the attributes of God are addressed throughout the year during prayer times. Only referring to God as one of "judgment and wrath" causes those needing to know God as "patient and loving" to quit participating in class prayer. A teacher must carefully monitor how they lead the class in prayer and how they address God.

THE TEACHER AT THE ALTAR

Students often observe their teachers during worship services. If they see their teacher help others pray at altar services, they note that the teacher lives what he teaches. On the other hand, if a teacher never prays with others at the altar, students will question the importance of prayer. Students will also observe how their teacher personally responds to altar calls. When they see their teacher praying for himself, they see the teacher acknowledging the power and need of prayer for everyone.

PRAYER IS THE NORM

Prayer is absolutely foundational for the Christian pilgrimage. When we meditate on the verse that tells us to "pray without ceasing," we understand even more clearly the importance of prayer and teaching on prayer. Yes, there are many other topics and doctrines that must be taught to our students. However, with creative methods, prayer can constantly be emphasized in the midst of teaching other topics. Hopefully our students will begin to see prayer and prayer time as the norm and not the exception. Just as the Master showed His disciples how to pray, we must teach our students to pray.

4

The Teacher's Practice of Prayer

by LeRoy Bartel

I would like to offer a tribute to my mother, Vera Shirley Bartel, one of the most effective teachers and praying Christians I know. Mom taught a Sunday school class for many years. Even after she retired, a young adult class begged her to be their teacher. Her lesson preparation was bathed in prayer. I remember her throwing herself across her bed on Sunday afternoons with her Bible and hearing prayer sounds come out of the bedroom all afternoon long as she began preparations for her class the coming Sunday.

Mom believed battles were won and spiritual progress was made around the prayer altars of our church. She was at every service, praying individually with the members of her class as they waged spiritual warfare. If she became aware of a special problem or struggle a particular student was facing, his difficulty became her personal prayer project. She would pray daily and fervently until the battle was won. I vividly remember a particular prayer project she tackled. Satan was trying to destroy a marriage. She clenched her delicate, feminine fists and her jaw and said, "Satan will not get this one!" And he didn't.

Today Mom and Dad are retired and are in their eighties. They still receive telephone calls requesting prayer. Mornings, in their modest home, are dedicated entirely to prayer ministry. Name after name, prayer project after prayer project, missionary after missionary, minister after minister, and nation after nation are all part of their prayers on any given day.

Mom's impact upon the world has not been as a theologian. Her impact, however, as a godly woman of prayer, would be difficult to calculate! She has served as a model for the prayer ministry of hundreds of Christians, including her sons. Prayer has always been an integral and indispensable part of her ministry as a teacher.

Each one of us knows someone who has made a significant impact on our lives with prayer. Our lives will never be the same because of them. We saw in their lives a dynamic, created by their communion with God, that arouses within us the desire to be godly, effective, praying people.

PERSONAL PRIORITY OF THE TEACHER'S PRAYER

Teachers who are effective in teaching prayer are teachers who pray! The practice of prayer must become a priority in the teacher's life for it to become important in the student's life. It is not enough for the teacher to know about prayer, to have read books about prayer, or even to emphasize its importance in class sessions. The teacher who attempts to teach prayer must pray!

The teacher cannot be successful by eternal measurement and appraisal without prayer. Prayer is the lifeline, the channel of divine power and potential for effective ministry as a teacher. Effective Christian teachers realize that prayer is a critical element in productive ministry.

Prayer must become a continual habit of life. It begins with a constant awareness of God in all of life. It progresses with a grateful spirit and a continual attitude of worship and praise. Prayer expresses the teacher's relationship with God and becomes the context in which that relationship is nurtured.

God's Word refers to a continual, inner prayer of the Spirit in the believer's life. Paul encouraged believers to "pray without ceasing"(1 Thessalonians 5:17). This continual "spirit of prayer" becomes a powerful context for effective ministry—the wellspring from which effectiveness flows.

Prayer must become a priority in the Christian teacher's daily life. It is something he does because he cannot do without it. He will allow nothing to push it out of his life. Neither hectic schedules, nor the pressures of daily living, are permitted to preempt it. Effective Christian teachers make time for it.

Prayer needs to be the first thing of our day and the last thing we do at night. David captured this dynamic when he said, "It is good to praise the Lord and...to proclaim your love in the morning and your faithfulness at night" (Psalm 92:1,2).

Jesus set the tone for the priority of prayer in a teacher's life. At times Jesus "continued all night in prayer" (Luke 6:12; Mark 6:45–48). At other times He awoke early after an exhausting day of ministry the previous day and prayed (Mark 1:35). He prayed to prepare for the crises and significant events of His ministry (Matthew 14:23; Mark 1:35–39; Luke 3:21,22; 9:18–22). He prayed to prepare himself for the temptation He saw coming (Luke 22:39–45). He prayed about the most ordinary matters of daily life (Matthew 14:19; Luke 24:30,31). He prayed standing (John 11:41,42), kneeling (Luke 22:41), and lying on His face (Matthew 26:39). The last utterance of His earthly life was a prayer (Luke 23:34, 46). Can the Christian teacher today do less than follow the example set by the Master Teacher?

PRINCIPLES TO GUIDE THE TEACHER'S PRAYER

For a teacher's prayer life to have "teaching impact" several principles should guide his personal communion with God.

Prepared

There are several attitudes and practices that prepare the Christian teacher for effective prayer. An awareness of God's presence is indispensable to powerful prayer. Reverence ought to captivate our minds and hearts—we ought to take time to be aware of who God really is (Psalm 46:10). Praise, worship, and thanksgiving provide a dynamic atmosphere for prayer (Psalm 100). The combination of these "door–openers" to God's presence makes our time spent with Him count!

Personal

Powerful prayer is neither characterized by fancy words nor ostentatious phrases. It flows out of a personal relationship with God. It focuses on a person and is expressed in sincerity of heart. We are talking to "Our Father" and our prayer ought to characterize the reality of that relationship (Matthew 6:5–13).

Positive

Dynamic praying expresses faith. The confidence that God cares, that God is able, that God is willing, and that God will act, ought to permeate our praying (Matthew 7:9–11; Mark 11:22–24; Hebrews 11:6). Our prayers ought to express hope and confidence in God. This kind of attitude is contagious!

Powerful

Don't pray so that you put yourself to sleep. Wake up and talk to God from your heart! There is an appropriate authority, one not presumptuous or arrogant, to be expressed in prayer. We come to God "in Jesus' name" (John 14:12,13; 16:23,24). Fervency and conviction in prayer are natural by-products of a vital relationship with God (Acts 12:5). The last thing your students need to hear is boring, listless prayer.

Pervasive and perpetual

Prayer should impregnate every part of our lives. A casual reading of Acts or a review of the history of Pentecostal churches will reveal a common trait—these people prayed about everything! The Bible admonishes us to do the same (Philippians 4:6,7). Imagine what vitality would be brought back to the Church if we would simply "pray about everything, all of the time"!

Persistent

One of the most striking things about great "pray-ers" has been their persistence in prayer. These people refuse to give up. They are not trying to overcome God's reluctance; rather, they know how to lay hold of this willingness (Matthew 7:7, 8). This is exactly the attitude Jesus commended in the Parable of the Unjust Judge (Luke 18:1–8). Such prayer does not display a lack of faith; rather, it expresses strength of trust in God.

Purposeful

Christian teachers should determine to accomplish something when they pray. Prayer must never simply become "putting in time." Jesus rebuked an attitude like that and assured His disciples that they had the ear and concern of a loving Father (Matthew 6:7,8). Our praying should be simple, direct, and focused.

Paraclete-assisted

One of the greatest joys for a Pentecostal believer is the awareness of the role the Holy Spirit plays in prayer. The Holy Spirit helps us express our love and praise to God (1 Corinthians 14:2,14–19; Acts 2:7–11). He also prays through us when we do not know how to pray. He will groan intercessions through us to God in keeping with God's will (Romans 8:26,27). May we never lose this dynamic in our prayer ministry as teachers!

PERSONAL PRACTICE OF THE TEACHER'S PRAYER

A rich variety ought to characterize a teacher who models an effective prayer life. Christian teachers must know how to pray in a variety of settings and ways. They should not get into a rut, but be able to participate meaningfully in various kinds of prayer with other believers. Their lives ought be characterized by a balance of prayer's various components. Paul felt strongly about this. He urged believers in his closing charge in Ephesians: "Pray in the Spirit on all occasions with all kinds of prayers and requests. With this in mind, be alert and always keep on praying for all the saints. Pray also for me, that whenever I open my mouth, words may be given me so that I will fearlessly make known the mystery of the gospel" (Ephesians 6:18,19). Students should be able to observe a variety and balance in the prayer practices of their teacher so they can learn from and desire to emulate him.

Practicing Personal Prayer

There is no excuse for a teacher to neglect personal prayer. It is the wellspring from which effective ministry flows. Time must be made for personal prayer in the teacher's daily schedule. We minister out of the reservoir of our lives, and if the reservoir is empty or polluted we become personally ineffective and a risk to others. Neglecting a personal time with God is to practice spiritual anorexia, expose oneself to debilitating spiritual disease, and invite spiritual disaster and death. Why would we neglect prayer when the door to fellowship with the Living God stands open at all times?

Balance must be maintained in our personal prayer. Becoming aware and sensitive to God's presence, offering personal praise and worship, confessing sin and personal spiritual need, maintaining balance between personal petition and intercession, offering thanks, and the all important discipline of listening to God's voice must all be a part of our personal prayer. We must be alert to the fact that our public and corporate praying will only be as effective as our personal practice of prayer.

Practicing Corporate Prayer

What an encouragement and blessing it is to pray with other believers! When the gathered assembly of believers lift their voices to God in petition and praise, the effect is contagious. The power of God is sensed, and the faith of others seems to lift and encourage our expression of confidence in God. God has promised to be with His people when they gather in His name. The Christian teacher should determine not to neglect the various corporate prayer opportunities of the church.

Small group prayer also provides a tremendous opportunity; for the teacher must learn how to meaningfully participate in corporate prayer. The practice of "conversational prayer"—individuals simply speaking out to God in praise, petition, confession, and thanksgiving while others agree with them in prayer—is a wonderful experience. The group is bonded together, God's presence is felt, and miracles often happen.

Practicing Public Prayer

Public prayer is often not taught. Few receive help in how to "lead in prayer" or guidance regarding how to meaningfully participate when someone is leading in prayer. Those who lead in prayer should sincerely and thoughtfully, but forcefully "lead out" in a prayer on behalf of the entire congregation or class and its needs. The rest of the congregation or class should alertly listen and verbally affirm and agree with what is being articulated. It should not be a case of everyone "praying their own thing."

Second Chronicles 6:12 to 7:3, the account of Solomon's powerful prayer at the dedication of the temple, illustrates the possibilities of properly leading in prayer. The Bible says that when Solomon prayed "all the Israelites saw the fire coming down and the glory of the Lord above the temple, they knelt on the pavement with their faces to the ground, and they worshiped and gave thanks to the Lord" (7:3). Teachers in our churches must learn how to "lead in prayer" and model it effectively.

Practicing Prayer Ministry With Individuals

Personal prayer ministry with individuals in the church who have needs is undoubtedly one of the most effective forms of ministry a teacher can have. The prayer services that are regularly held at the close of a service provide unbelievable opportunities for a teacher to be a blessing. Teachers should be alert to students from their class who are at the altar and be there to pray with them. Altar calls in a kid's crusade, a vacation Bible school, or children's church provide prime opportunities to see God do something marvelous in a child's life. It is always appropriate to take a moment, visit with the person who has come forward for prayer, and seek to determine what they need or want from God. A teacher cannot afford to neglect any of these opportunities to pray with others.

Teachers must develop the personal habit of suggesting prayer when they become aware of a student's need. It is so easy to think only in terms of formal prayer opportunities. When a student, young or old, expresses a need anywhere, at any time, it is appropriate to ask, "May I pray with you about that?" This may not only take place in church. Some of the most effective personal prayer ministry takes place in a home, at a restaurant, or in a conversation on the street. God has always delighted in pouring His blessing out on the spontaneous situation in answer to believing prayer. Early believers proved that He was God of the marketplace!

Practicing Unselfish Prayer

A disease that seems to have infected the entire human race since the sin of the first parents is selfishness. Tragically, the effect of this sin seems to have influenced even the way we pray. The fact is, it is so easy for us to slip into a pattern of "me, mine, and ours" in prayer: "Lord, meet my needs, satisfy our desires, bless our church, etc." Only a deep and radical work of the Spirit of God can change our prayer focus. God calls us to lay aside our personal concerns and seek first His kingdom and His righteousness. He assures us, that if we do, everything else we need will be given to us as well (Matthew 6:33). The heart of God throbs for the people of the world, the sin of humanity, and the festering needs of hurting man. May the students we teach pick up the heartthrob of God for others from our praying! Jesus calls Christian teachers to be "others-oriented" in their prayers.

Practicing Prayer In The Classroom

The classrooms in our churches must become more than just formal places of instruction—they must become "prayer zones," designated places of prayer. God desires for the buildings we have dedicated to Him to truly become "houses of prayer" (Matthew 21:12,13).

Teachers must be prepared to lead in a variety of prayer dynamics and activities that provide instruction and experience in prayer, as well as a dynamic atmosphere in which God can act powerfully in lives. These activities should be age-level sensitive and planned to provide a variety of prayer experiences with a balanced view of prayer. This can only take place if the teacher has a balanced and varied personal prayer life.

POSSIBILITIES OF MODELED PRAYER

I remember standing as a young boy of 10 or 11 years of age in an evening "fellowship meeting" service at Bigfork, Montana. The services that day had been long and most of the people in attendance were older Christians. There was really little in the service to appeal to an adolescent. We stood for prayer time and an old German man was asked to lead us in prayer. From the moment the old man began to pray, everything in that service took on new meaning to me.

I had never heard anyone pray like that before. The old man just stood there and carried on a very personal and powerful conversation with the Living God. Through simple, but profound, broken English he poured out his heart to God. I was awestruck! I had never heard praying like that in my life. I found my heart saying, "Oh God, I want to pray like that!" I never got away from that prayer.

One of the most potent tools available to the teacher for the faith-formation of others is his own life.

We teach through the grid of our lives—who we are, what we believe, and what we do. The teacher's personal prayer life provides a model for others to learn from and emulate.

Jesus exemplifies the potential and power of the teacher's personal prayer life for teaching prayer. One day Jesus' disciples watched Him as He prayed in a certain unnamed place. We don't know what they saw Him do or what they heard Him say. It must have been a powerful experience, however, for when He finished His disciples said to Him, "Lord, teach us to pray" (Luke 11:1). Somehow I believe their experience that day must have been a bit like the experience I had as a boy in Bigfork, Montana. Jesus demonstrated that day the powerful impact a teacher's prayer life can have on his students.

There are at least six areas where the powerful influence of the teacher's prayer can be seen.

- *The teacher will sense the change that prayer makes on his own life.*

There will be a new discovery of power and fellowship with God that nourishes his service for the Lord. Students will sense the change and respond positively.

- *There will be a powerful effect on teaching.*

Lessons prepared prayerfully are communicated with power. The dynamics of the teacher's prayer will bleed over into the classroom and influence everything that happens there. There will be a refreshing creativity that never existed before. Prayer dynamics will become a part of classroom activities.

- *Prayer will begin to have an influence on students.*

They may not know why, but they will experience a new openness to God and His will for their lives. There will be a new interest in the Word of God. Lives will be changed. Students will begin to see and desire the life of devotion and prayer exemplified by the teacher.

- *The teacher's prayer will have an effect on situations in the class and in the lives of the students.*

God answers prayer, and He will hear the sincere requests of a teacher regarding the needs in his class. How exciting it is as a teacher to see God begin to answer prayer!

- *The teacher's praying will have a positive benefit for the church.*

Whenever God's people begin to pray, things begin to happen in the church. People are convinced of their need for God and are saved, a new dimension of spiritual vitality comes to the congregation, and an attitude of unity and love prevails among God's people—a congregation experiences revival!

- *There is an impact that is felt in the world.*

God desires to manifest His glory and power in this evil world. He is not willing that any should perish (2 Peter 3:9). God is raising up an army of intercessors who will pray earnestly for those who are spiritually blind.

CONCLUSION

Several months ago in a Bible college chapel service I heard a challenging message on the subject of intercessory prayer. As I listened, I was suddenly struck forcibly by the questions, "Who will take the place of intercessors like my mother?" and "Who will serve as the models of prayer for the coming generation?"

That day, with tears running down my face, I purposed to perpetuate the legacy of prayer I had received. I determined to be a model of prayer for my generation. I resolved to teach prayer by example.

Will you?

5

Commitment Is More Than a Catch Word

by Larry Thomas

Dr. Kenneth Gangel described this present generation as well as anyone can by saying, "The one thing that marks this generation is that they are totally committed to not being committed to anything."[8] We can all agree that it's a very different time. The rapid advances in communications, technology, access to easy world travel, and the sweeping revolutionary changes in the most remote parts of the globe have brought about changes that affect every part of our lives and society. The church has not escaped these changes.

Just a few years ago it was easy to offer a nice, neat package that fit neatly into the life-styles of almost everyone in the local community. The typical work week was 40 hours with weekends off. To find a business or a store that stayed open all night or on Sundays was next to impossible.

But all of that has changed. Shift work is now the norm. Days off come in the middle of the week. The community concept of living has been abandoned for privacy and seclusion (which is being labeled as cocooning). Housing developments now offer secured surroundings with guards posted at the entrance. It seems that most homes now place an "unwelcome" mat at the front door.

As a result of these changes, every phase of our society has been affected: the school system, the workplace, the family, and the church. Leaders are being forced to look for new ways to adapt to the changes or else face severe problems.

The church is not exempt from this process. It must respond accordingly by looking for new and more effective methods to reach an ever-changing market with the never-changing message. According to a church analyst, the future of the church looks bleak if the present structure is maintained.

The analyst further believes that the church is beginning to experience selective attendance patterns by its adherents who will only attend if they feel immediate needs are being met. He also predicts a decline in loyalty to denominations, a decreasing number who desire to commit to membership in a local church, a growing number of teachers and workers who will not commit for more than a few weeks, and an overall lackadaisical attitude toward the church and all other organizations together.

Leith Anderson put it this way: "Modern American culture places great emphasis on self, independence, and personal fulfillment. Combined with mobility and uncertainty, these trends make long-term commitments seem inappropriate. This is a phenomenon that is having a major impact on our institutions."[9]

There are many factors that have created this scenario. Anderson lists such things as our mobility, increasing numbers of ethnic groups, the aging of the population, shifting values, and the tendency towards short-term commitments.

We can all agree that the church is facing a monumental task, yet it is to this generation that Jesus said, "Go and make disciples of all nations" (Matthew 28:19).

THE NEED FOR DISCIPLESHIP

When we look at the trends that are developing, we must agree that there is a great need for a rebirth of discipleship in the local church. Discipleship is the means that enables an organization to perpetuate itself from generation to generation.

Organizations are no longer guaranteed a life span beyond the present generation. No longer can they exist on a hand-me-down loyalty. Just because we belong to a denomination is no assurance that our children will. Anderson said, "Children are now less likely to follow in their parents' denominational footsteps, meaning that the loyalty of each new generation must be won rather than inherited." The process of discipleship holds the key to reversing these trends as well as many other ones. It is a safe assumption that if the Church is to be an effective force in the world as we enter the 21st-century, discipleship and commitment must be stressed.

BENEFITS OF DISCIPLESHIP

Discipleship is a training process. Through the discipleship process a new convert can be directed through the growth and maturity process that is necessary to become an effective member of the kingdom of God. Without discipleship, the chances of a new convert making it are pretty slim.

Just as a child needs parental love, nurture, guidance, and direction to successfully reach adulthood, a new convert needs systematic training to develop into an effective Christian worker. Discipleship helps him recognize and avoid the snares and dangers that dot the road to maturity.

Discipleship provides growth. Findley B. Edge, in his book *Teaching For Results*, says that people are saved at the point of their conviction. By this he means that when a person hears a sermon dealing with some aspect of their lives, they are convicted and often respond by asking for forgiveness. Yet that same person may still have a number of bad habits and do things that are not Christlike. The discipleship process provides opportunities for the Holy Spirit to work in all areas of a person's life, helping him grow spiritually and conform to the image of Christ.

Discipleship provides training. The discipleship process is invaluable for providing on-the-job training for aspiring Christian workers. Someone once pointed out that Jesus had only 3 years to reach the world with His gospel, so He chose 12 men. These 12 men, who were discipled and trained for the office of apostle, had the privilege of walking with Jesus during His earthly life. He chose these so "that they might be with Him" (Mark 3:14). These men, ranging from fishermen to tax collectors, watched and listened to Jesus as He faithfully carried out the plan of God on a day-to-day basis. They learned by what they observed and heard.

This is what discipleship is all about, investing your life in the lives of others, equipping them for ministry. When Jesus left that small band of men, they were suddenly thrust into service. But the record shows that they were ready. By spending time with them, Jesus developed a ministry team that "turned the world upside down" (Act 17:6, KJV).

Discipleship facilitates assimilation. Assimilation is the process of blending in and becoming a part of a group. In today's society people are always on the move. Some statistics show that the average church member changes churches every 3–5 years. This means finding and making new friends, finding new places of service, and having to blend in church social life.

Newcomers often find it very difficult to become an integral part of the local church. But, if a church will take time to develop a discipleship program for both the newcomer and the new convert, it will enjoy a higher success rate in maintaining new people.

THE PROCESS OF DISCIPLESHIP

The Greeks were great lovers of philosophy. The concept of disciples originated within the Greek culture. Greeks like Aristotle spent many hours developing new "schools of thought."

Teachers would expound their philosophies in hopes of attracting disciples who would follow them and perpetuate their teaching. Often they would develop large crowds of followers who would be "their disciples." These loyal followers would sit for hours listening to the teachers, and attaching themselves to them and their philosophies.

This was so much a part of their culture that it was reflected in their vocabulary. *Disciple* comes from the Greek word *mathetes*, meaning "a learner or one who follows one's teaching." The contrasting word is *didaskalos* or "teacher." Hence the word *disciple* denotes "one who follows one's teaching."

The concept of teacher/follower carried over into the Jewish culture. The Bible refers to those who were disciples of Moses (John 9:28). The Pharisees developed out of this group of disciples. John the Baptist had his followers or disciples (Matthew 9:14). At one point, he relinquished some of his disciples to become followers of Christ (John 1:35–37).

It was only natural that Jesus would have disciples, too. However, His approach was different from all the rest. His was a discipleship based on a relationship with the person. He simply called them so that they could be with Him.

John 6, gives us an insight into the way Jesus made disciples. First, we see that His followers were curiosity seekers (John 6:1–14). They had seen Him do great miracles, they had been a part of the multitude He had fed, and they discovered He had gone to the other side of the lake without a boat. They rushed to the other side to find out how He did this (John 6:24, 25).

This mentality still exists today. It is easy to draw a crowd with a spectacular event. However, commitment and discipleship go far beyond being a curiosity seeker.

Jesus' second step was to lead them beyond the curiosity stage, teaching them who He was and building their faith in His teachings (John 6:35–59). Each person must develop a personal relationship with the Lord. This decision is more than just being curious about a "miracle worker," but based on who He is and what He desires for our lives.

Many people have problems with this phase of discipleship. It's fine to enjoy the excitement and benefits of Christianity, but taking up the cross is a different thing (John 6:60). It's at this point that a person proceeds to the final step of commitment or backs away altogether. In our society, when people hear the cost, it is easy to follow the example of those early disciples who "turned back and no longer followed him" (John 6:66).

The ultimate goal of the discipleship process is an unwavering commitment. Peter's response to Jesus' probing question sums it up so well, "Lord, to whom shall we go?" (John 6:68).

DISCIPLESHIP FROM THE PENTECOSTAL PERSPECTIVE

The discipleship process must include preserving the Pentecostal distinctive that has made such an impact around the world. Church history shows that when a movement loses it distinctive, it becomes just another church organization.

The discipling of new converts, denominational crossovers, or those born into the church must include an awareness that Pentecostalism is more than emotions, excitement, or "spectacularism." Rather, it is an experience that empowers and equips believers to have power over sin, demons, and devils.

If we ever lose the gift of healing, the hope of the Rapture, the confidence in the Blood, and the baptism of the Holy Spirit evidenced by speaking in tongues, we will indeed become an anemic church that has lost its effectiveness in the world.

Pentecostal discipling will insure that we will always have a unique experience instead of just a unique doctrine.

SUNDAY SCHOOL'S ROLE IN DISCIPLESHIP

The Church faces a great challenge. The good news is that the Christian education ministry of the local church is a vehicle already in place to expedite the commission to make disciples.

Christian education is an umbrella term that can be used to refer to all the nurturing ministries of the church. By nurturing, we mean those programs specifically designed for the age, peer, and interest groups that comprise the local church.

Included under this umbrella would be the various specialized programs such as children's church, Missionettes, Royal Rangers, and Sunday School. You can also include Youth, Men's, and Women's Ministries. In essence, any group that promotes training and spiritual growth is a nurturing ministry.

According to George Edgerly, national secretary of the Sunday School Promotion and Training Department, "The most effective of all is Sunday school." He bases his statement on the scope of the Sunday school rather than its impact.

All other programs in the church are directed at specific target groups. Sunday school is directed at the entire family. There is a place in Sunday school for everyone from birth until death. A person never outlives the scope of a well-designed and administered Sunday school. Here are three important factors that make Sunday school a powerful tool for discipleship.

The Structure

The structure of the Sunday school is its greatest strength. Elmer Towns, a leading authority on Sunday school, defines the structure in three parts: "The reaching, teaching, and discipling arm of the church."

The basic strength of the Sunday school is its small group dynamics. Good things happen in small groups. It has been proven over and over that small groups are ideal learning environments. In small groups, individuality is not lost. The teacher has time to interact with all students and build relationships with them.

Small groups provide intimate settings so each person can develop a sense of belonging. It is a setting in which the individuals develop their own relationships and make new friends. It is also much easier to assimilate a person into the church if it is done in a small group setting.

Group dynamics facilitate outreach and evangelism. Prospective members are more likely to join a small group first. The reason is that most people feel uncomfortable in a large crowd where they do not know anyone. Have you ever gone to a function and found that you knew absolutely no one in the crowd? You were probably rather uncomfortable.

The small group is also ideal for discipleship. A person's growth and development can be easily monitored. Within the safety of the group, mistakes and failures can occur without devastating the person; group support and reinforcement are available. Group members can also be discipleship role models.

Groups provide a sense of community. Sunday schools are generally grouped around people who have the same interests, needs, and approximate age. This is a positive factor in discipleship. A person can learn and benefit from the experiences of others in the group. This common group focuses on needs, problems, and solutions unique to its stage of life. In the process, individuals deepen their lives and help disciple one another.

The Teacher

Without a good teacher, discipleship does not happen. The teacher is more than a transmitter of knowledge. A teacher is a people builder and a mentor. He accomplishes this task by investing his life in the lives of his students, helping them mature, becoming more Christlike in their everyday lives. There are five distinguishable marks of an effective teacher.

The Teacher Is A Role Model

The greatest lesson a teacher can learn is that his teaching is not in the classroom only, but everywhere he goes. A teacher can rarely lead his students to a degree of discipleship greater than his own. Regardless of what a teacher presents in the classroom, an inconsistency on the outside will negate most of what is taught. A teacher who is unwilling to accept this responsibility needs to cease teaching.

A Teacher Is A Learner

If a teacher is successful at discipling those in his class, then most likely the teacher is an avid student of the Bible and other materials that help him become a better teacher. The most exciting teachers are those who have first been excited by what they are going to teach.

The learning process involves proper training. A good teacher will avail himself of every training opportunity that presents itself. Natural talents, longevity of service, or experience do not decrease the need for ongoing training.

A teacher who is not a learner soon bankrupts his resources. It's the same principal as having a checking account. If a person continues to write checks without making deposits, a time will come when the resources are depleted. It's true that when a teacher ceases to learn, he ceases to teach.

A Teacher Is A Patient Person

A teacher has to review the same principles time and again. Sometimes it seems as if the students will never understand what is trying to be communicated. Then one day it happens. You see that look on the student's face. He understands! Then the first question he usually asks is, "Why didn't you tell me this before?" A teacher must remember that discipleship is a process that takes patience and time. Looking back over the 3 years Jesus spent training His disciples reveals several frustrating times with them. But what men they turned out to be. A good teacher never loses sight of the ultimate goal—discipleship.

A Teacher Has A Mission

A good teacher is driven by something higher than extrinsic rewards. A teacher has been called of God and is motivated by a desire to make disciples of everyone who comes under his teaching ministry. Dr. Howard G. Hendricks verbalized this concept well. He said, "Teaching that impacts is not head to head, but heart to heart."

A Teacher Looks For Teaching Opportunities

Discipling involves spending time with people. Therefore, a good teacher is always looking for ways to reinforce his teaching. For example, a teacher of a primary class always takes a student or two with her when she visits a sick student.

On the way she talks about what the Bible says about praying for the sick and healing. She has the other children help her pray for their sick classmate. After the visit, she takes them home to discuss what they have done. These are lessons that can never be taught in the classroom alone. It is discipleship in its purest form.

The Curriculum

The curriculum is as important as the teacher. Curriculum is to discipleship what a proper diet is to the body. In essence, what you eat is what you are.

Over the past several years there has been a tendency to teach lessons and subjects that were trendy or appealed to special interest. Although this is not wrong, it carries a certain degree of inherent danger.

The curriculum we choose should meet certain qualifications. It must be sound. Discipleship does not occur where weak, anemic ideas and philosophies are taught. Growth can only occur when sound doctrine is taught. (See Titus 2:1.)

Curriculum must be balanced. More and more people today are experiencing health problems that can be directly traced back to poor eating habits. By the same token, how many of the problems in the church can be traced to unbalanced teaching?

A balanced curriculum has a tremendous impact on the discipleship process. It takes the learner on a structured cycle of learning that covers the entire scope of the Bible. Granted, some parts will be less interesting than others, but some vegetables aren't as enjoyable as double cheese pizza, but they are necessary for proper growth.

It must emphasize doctrinal distinctive. What we ignore we lose. If we fail to indoctrinate the new converts and our children, we stand to lose a great deal. Discipleship should always include teaching what we believe and why. Curriculum choice plays a vital role in discipleship. The choice should be a Pentecostal-based curriculum that is not hesitant to include the Pentecostal doctrines. Otherwise, we have no sure way of perpetuating this experience in the coming generations. Curriculum must not be selected by its looks, cost, or ease of use, but by its teachings.

CONCLUSION

What does the future hold? What place will the church have in the future? How effective will the church be in the 21st century? All of these are perplexing questions that no one can answer for sure.

The reason for the uncertainty is the answer has not yet been decided. Every denomination, organization, and church is granted the opportunity to decide its place in the overall plan of

God. Churches can stay strong and effective or become weak and anemic. The question is not what will happen to the church but what will be our place in the church. The church will survive with or without us.

To enjoy long-term effectiveness, the Church must maintain the proper relationship with the Head of the Church, Jesus Christ. It must also maintain doctrinal purity, a passionate desire to win the lost, and a keen awareness of its overall mission.

Next, the Church must do everything it can to perpetuate itself from generation to generation. What this means is that every generation must encourage and instruct the next generation to seek out its own experience rather than relying upon a second-generation experience. To faithfully do so will keep us from experiencing what Israel experienced: "Another generation grew up, who knew neither the Lord nor what he had done for Israel. Then the Israelites did evil in the eyes of the Lord and served Baals" (Judges 2:10,11).

The way to do this is simple: make disciples of all men. Perhaps this is the burden David felt. His request was "Even when I am old and gray, do not forsake me, O God, till I declare your power to the next generation, your might to all who are to come" (Psalm 71:18).

6

Follow-up:
The "Keeping" Ministry
of the Church

by Efraim Espinoza

Therefore go and make disciples of all nations, baptizing
them in the name of the Father and of the Son and of the
Holy Spirit, and teaching them to obey everything I have
commanded you. And surely I am with you always, to the
very end of the age (Matthew 28:19,20).

We are born to grow. This is the first fact of life discovered
by those who decide to follow the Lord. God's Word to man
in Jesus Christ was and is—"Let's get growing."—Robert
Domeij[10]

The evangelical church has continued to show remarkable
growth in the last decade of the 20th century. Megachurches are
scheduling multiple services to accommodate the crowds. Lively
music, excellent praise and worship, and dynamic preaching
are attracting the crowds. The baby boomer generation is
returning to church.

Even in political circles, being "born again" can have a
dramatic impact on the outcome of elections. Current issues like
pro-life/pro-choice or homosexuality in the military have pro-
vided a platform for the evangelical perspective to be brought to
the forefront. On occasions, local and national leaders have
sought the support of Christians on controversial issues to
ensure passage of legislation.

Notwithstanding, the commitment factor of the modern evangelical has seemingly dwindled. Keith Drury describes this present day situation in the following way:

> We've had a growing new class of Christians in the last decade or so. This is the fastest growing type of Christian today. They are the 'unconverted converted' or the 'secular Christian' as some scholars call them. These folk claim to be saved, but don't let religion cramp their style. They are consumers, moving through churches as they would a salad bar, picking and choosing what appeals to them, and leaving the rest alone. They generally select the positive, helpful, pleasant benefits of the gospel and leave the painful, sacrificial, cross-carrying, and judgment aspects. They are a shallow bunch and a happy lot.[11]

The Church must return to ministry that can address this issue in a systematic approach without succumbing to the tendency of establishing a new program. It must be a ministry that encompasses obedience to the discipleship aspect of the Great Commission. It is the Church's responsibility to disciple believers so that evangelism can continue from generation to generation until Jesus' return.

Sunday school is the Church in obedience to the Great Commission! The mandate in Matthew 28:19,20; Mark 16:15; and other passages clearly indicates the mission of the Church to—

- Go—that's evangelism and outreach.
- Baptize—that's assimilation.
- Teach—that's incorporation.

Without developing a new program or a new ministry, the local Sunday school can provide the framework within the church for evangelism, assimilation, and incorporation. Properly functioning, Sunday school is the reaching and keeping ministry of the church.

DISCIPLESHIP BY DESIGN

Spiritual development or discipleship can be described as the process of guiding an individual from being an unbeliever to salvation (new convert), to becoming a member of a local church through the equipping process (training), so that he can actively serve in the ministry of his local church. The apostle Paul, in writing to the church in Ephesus, reminds them that, by design, the role of leadership gifts in the church is to equip the saints "for the work of the ministry, for the edifying of the body of Christ" (Ephesians 4:12, KJV). By definition, Sunday school is

> the evangelistic and educational ministry which groups individuals by age, school grade, and/or interest for weekly study of God's Word. The Sunday school provides the church with a teaching ministry to reach, teach, win the individual to Christ, and to disciple and train him for Christian service.[12]

By design, Sunday school is the "small group" ministry of the church for all ages, not just adult fellowship groups.

By encompassing all age groups, Sunday school provides the local congregation the structure for accountability of active and potential attenders. Also, the local Sunday school can provide both systematic record keeping and expansion through the addition of new classes or departments. It is discipleship through assimilation and incorporation.

Assimilation

Assimilation is defined as the process of "making similar." To assimilate is to receive new people into the church and accept them as being like the rest. The church's mission is to be a living body of believers, bound together by strong ties of fellowship and brotherhood. Assimilation will take place when relationship is a major concern of the local church. The format of small groups (classes) in Sunday school builds bridges of friendship and relationships that are not easily accessible in the worship experience. Friendship is one of the most important keys in binding newcomers to each other and to the church.

Addressing this topic in *Hey, That's Our Church*, Lyle E. Schaller writes, "The 'belonging factor' is of major importance in understanding the process of assimilation."[13]

It is true that the major thrust of Sunday school is the systematic teaching of God's Word. Yet, it is the friendship factor, relationships with others, that spurs continued participation and involvement in Sunday school.

Incorporation

Incorporation is the process of integrating newcomers into the body of believers. The process involves more than just making newcomers feel welcomed. By design, the Sunday school increases the potential for incorporation in the following ways:

1. It provides more opportunities for service and involvement. Each class has a teacher, class secretary, and substitute or team teacher, along with other opportunities for areas of hospitality, visitation (follow-up), coordination, and fellowship.

2. The addition of new classes encourages homogeneous small groups (classes) within the heterogeneous body (the church). Newcomers are more likely to become participants in a new group than an already established group.

3. The process of developing new classes also recognizes the fact that each class has a saturation point at which it can no longer assimilate and incorporate new people. Survey results substantiate the fact that Sunday school classes have a "saturation point" beyond which they cannot grow.[14]

Church growth specialists have consistently offered two simple, proven principles concerning the addition or deletion of classes in the local Sunday school. These principles are: "merging existing classes inhibits growth," and "establishing new classes encourages growth."

Discipleship is a reality when the local Sunday school leadership makes a consistent effort at both assimilation and incorporation. It is Sunday school functioning at its optimum.

DISCIPLESHIP BY DIRECTION

The role of leadership is to effectively set an example of discipling by a consistent effort to improve the effectiveness of the local Sunday school. Theory alone will not produce a Sunday school that grows through follow-up. The goal of a discipling Sunday school is clearly communicated by the local leadership to the volunteer staff, to the regular attenders, to newcomers, and to prospective attenders.

The executive Sunday school officers and the entire Sunday school must enunciate the message that as a "discipling" Sunday school, they want to—

1. Reach new people. It is only in reaching new people that prospects for salvation and discipleship are clearly identified.

2. Set "outreach" or enrollment goals for each teaching unit. Unmarked targets are never hit. Goal-setting that is specific, attainable, and measurable will provide each class with a focused approach to continued growth.

3. Continually discover new prospects. Working through the membership in each class will enhance the opportunities for laity to become involved in identifying new prospects for the local Sunday school. Laity involvement is discipleship. It is focusing the emphasis of leadership to equip the saints for the work of ministry (Ephesians 4:11,12).

4. Put in place a systematic plan for identifying and reaching prospects.

Certain basic Sunday school elements must be properly considered and implemented for effective assimilation and incorporation to occur in the local Sunday school. Leadership must exemplify commitment to these elements in order to provide a Sunday school structure that can effectively reach out and disciple. These Sunday school elements are basic principles that are constant and universal. They will work in different situations. Notwithstanding, the practices and methods needed to implement these basic elements must be tailored to each situation. These five basic elements include:

Organization and Administration

A Sunday school that fulfills its mission in evangelism and discipleship must have adequate organization and administration. Organization is putting individual parts and plans together to develop the whole picture of the ministry. Some of the tools needed to organize the local Sunday school include a written operational policy, an organizational flow chart, proper attendance record keeping, adequate funding, and appropriate financial reporting. Administration is the coordination of the various functions towards the same goals. Basic to good Sunday school administration are duly selected general officers, job descriptions, annual planning, and systematic evaluation.

Staffing and Training

A systematic approach for recruitment of staff should include written descriptions of the assignments, proper screening, training, and supervision. Opportunities for service are essential in the proper assimilation and incorporation of new people to the congregation. Sunday school leadership must make a conscious effort to maintain the proper ratio of workers to pupils.

Training develops people's gifts and abilities. It must occur prior to placement and continue through the tenure of the workers. Training will shape character and provide additional skills and knowledge for the volunteer workers.

Growth and Evangelism

These elements are basic to the ongoing function of the local congregation. Without these two elements, churches lose their reason for being. A growth mentality must begin with a spiritual awareness of the lostness of mankind and a recognition of the responsibility of believers to win others to Christ. Simple human strategies won't produce healthy church growth. It requires a spiritually compassionate vision and willing vessels desiring to serve God through the ministry of the local church.

Systematic canvassing of the community will provide church leaders important information that can be used to develop a mission statement and plan of action for the local congregation. The local Sunday school leaders must survey the community, identify needs, and provide ministries to meet those needs.

Facilities and Resources

The local Sunday school leadership must demonstrate a commitment to provide the needed space and resources necessary for an effective Sunday school ministry. This includes maintaining the space necessary for sanctuary and classroom seating that will be conducive to effective ministry. It is understood that it may not always be possible to adhere to the recommended space requirements. Nevertheless, every effort should be made to provide the needed classroom space for each age level in the local Sunday school. Maximum usage of available space to meet the needs of the local congregation may include multiple scheduling of classes or the use of available space away from the church property.

Resources such as curriculum, overhead projectors, audio and video recordings, books, and craft and learning center materials are tools to assist in the teaching process. Developing a resource center, providing adequate curriculum that systematically teaches our Pentecostal distinctive, such as *Radiant Life/Vida Nueva* curriculum, and other related Sunday school resources are the responsibilities of the executive committee.

An ongoing, clearly communicated strategy to provide needed resources and curriculum must be developed. Sharing this strategy with volunteers can motivate them to greater service. Evangelism and discipleship have a cost. It required God to give His only begotten Son. Needed facilities and resources that will allow ministries to communicate the gospel message to the community require an investment of time and money.

Ministries

Ministry is meeting the special needs of people in Jesus' name. Sunday school is the ideal place to develop ministries that meet the needs of individuals within the reach of the local church. Three key factors that must be considered in developing the various ministries of Sunday school include:

1. *Evangelism.* Sunday schools ministries must reach beyond the church membership roles. It must include outreach to the lost and needy, as well as to church members.

2. *Assimilation and incorporation.* Sunday school must consist of caring groups (classes) where individuals can be nurtured and accepted. They must cultivate and water the "soil" of the hearts of unbelievers and disciple new converts.

3. *Training.* The consistent, effective teaching of the Bible provides the basis for developing people for ministry. Recruitment and training are vital to the ongoing ministry of Sunday school. Trained and equipped Sunday school workers are the extension of the ministry of the pastor in the local community.

DIRECTIONS For the Decade of Harvest Sunday School booklet and the *DIRECTIONS For the Decade of Harvest Sunday School Kit* are based on the above-mentioned five elements. These tools provide Sunday school leaders with the resources necessary to have these elements properly functioning in the congregation. The booklet (#714–516) and the kit (#714–518) can be ordered from the Sunday School Promotion and Training Department, 1445 Boonville Avenue, Springfield, MO 65802.

DISCIPLESHIP IN ACTION

Church leadership is more than having a title. It must be confirmed by life-styles that reflect its teachings. Discipleship through assimilation and incorporation should be the natural outflow of local Sunday school ministry. Commitment to "follow-up" must be an integral part of the total Sunday school ministry and not merely the responsibility of each individual teacher.

THE CHURCH GROWTH SPIRAL: A STRATEGY FOR EFFECTIVE FOLLOW-UP

It has been stated and proven that the first step of biblical and effective church growth is to develop groups and relationships. In this setting, growth will occur naturally because the church should build people not programs. The *Church Growth Spiral* helps Sunday school and church leaders envision, evaluate, plan, organize, and develop the resources and people in the local congregation for balanced growth.

The *Church Growth Spiral* is based on Arthur Flake's principles for Sunday school growth. He introduced these principles in 1922 as basic concepts for an effective and growing Sunday school. Today, these concepts still form the basis for a consistent growing pattern. They are: (1) Locate the prospects, (2) Enlarge the organization, (3) Enlist and train workers, (4) Provide the space, and (5) Go after the people.

A unique feature of the *Growth Spiral* is that it is based on enrollment rather than on attendance. "Locating the prospects" is just expanding the enrollment. "Enlarging the organization" is the addition of new units to assimilate the prospects into the Sunday school. "Enlisting and training workers" is the discipling/training program of the Sunday school that equips the laity for successful incorporation. "Providing the space" is the successful use of available space to accommodate new teaching units that the *Growth Spiral* will produce. To "go after the people" is the successful follow-up of regular Sunday school attenders, absentees, and prospects.

Follow-up is a major feature of the *Growth Spiral*. Each class develops a "support staff" of care workers who do the weekly contacts of the entire class enrollment. The *Growth Spiral* "care givers" provide opportunities for class members to become involved in the assimilation and incorporation process. The ratio of one care giver for every five enrolled in the class makes the goal of contacting 50 percent of the enrollment achievable.

The *Growth Spiral Kit* (#714–898) is available from the Sunday School Promotion and Training Department, 1445 Boonville Avenue, Springfield, MO 65802.

According to Elton Trueblood,

> The church is intended as a concrete answer to the prayer that laborers be sent forth to the harvest. The company of Jesus is not people streaming to a shrine; and it is not people making up an audience for a speaker; it is laborers engaged in the harvesting task of reaching their perplexed and seeking brethren with something so vital that, if received, it will change their lives.[15]

Two key emphases in both the Early Church and the Protestant Reformation were salvation by faith alone and the priesthood of all believers. These key ingredients must continue to prevail if the modern day church is to grow in the 21st century.

The church needs discipleship that includes assimilation and incorporation. Sunday school has the structure to produce continued growth through effective follow-up—if the church is willing to follow up.

7

Planting Seeds of Faith in the Preschool Years

by Sharon Ellard

Young children grow fast. Many kinds of rapid growth occur quickly during the first 5 years of life. For example, during the first year of life, most babies triple in weight. Mentally, the average 1-year-old child moves from speaking with 3 or 4 "para-words" parents must interpret to using 1,600 words by age 2. Developmentally, during the first 5 years, children go from being completely dependent babies to being able to walk, run, eat, talk, draw, climb, help others, and keep going and going long after parents and teachers run out of energy.

Spiritually, children also grow quickly during preschool years. To the untrained eye, however, these early stages of faith, prayer, and commitment may seem almost unrecognizable or insignificant. Considering God's purpose for seeds is one way to think about the significance of emerging faith in children.

In Genesis we learn that God made seed-bearing fruit (Genesis 1:11,12). Each kind of seed reproduces its own kind of fruit, even though the seed bears little resemblance to its mature fruit. Just as a small, hard black seed has the potential to grow into a red, juicy apple, the initial "seeds" of faith, prayer, and commitment in young children can develop into mature Pentecostal faith. A person who had never cut into an apple and seen the seeds it contains might be very skeptical about believing that a fruit could grow from something that looks more like a pebble than a part of a plant. In the same way, some adults are skeptical about believing that a nursery worker's tender feeding of a baby in the church nursery could play a significant role in growing faith or that a kindergartner's acting out David slaying Goliath could strengthen budding commitment in the heart of a little boy.

In fact, some adult responses to early spiritual development parallel the event in Psalm 118:22: "The stone the builders rejected has become the capstone." This verse is a prophecy about Jesus, so how can it also illustrate early spiritual development? The builders in the verse didn't recognize how a stone with slanting sides could fit into the overall building plans. Sometimes dedicated Christians don't recognize the impact early church relationships and experiences will have on later development of faith and commitment. Just as the builders in Psalm 118 rejected the stone with slanting sides from use in the walls and foundations of the building, teachers and parents sometimes discount the role of early behavior in children's spiritual growth. And yet, early experiences that lead children to love, trust, and obey may be the spiritual capstones that support the whole structure of later faith and commitment. The capstone and the apple seed illustrations should encourage teachers and parents to ask the Holy Spirit to increase their awareness of how faith is beginning to form in each of the children they influence.

Apple seeds can also be used to illustrate another point of early spiritual growth. Do you know enough about apples to identify different varieties? Do you, for example, know the difference between Red Delicious, Jonathan, and Granny Smith apples? Now suppose someone gave you a handful of apple seeds and asked you to sort them into the different varieties of apples they would grow. Would you be able to identify and separate Jonathan apple seeds from Granny Smith or Red Delicious seeds? I'm sure I wouldn't know one apple seed from another. Even if I noticed some small differences in the appearance of the different seeds, I still wouldn't know which would grow into Rome apples and which would develop into other varieties.

The Christian faith that develops during early childhood represents basic Christianity. Just as Jesus' disciples spent 3 years learning the basics about the kingdom of God from Him, young children will spend the first years of their lives learning the basics about God, Jesus, the Bible, and church. What a preschool child learns in a Bible-believing, evangelical Baptist church is going to closely parallel what another preschooler learns in a Spirit-filled Assembly of God Sunday school. Both children will learn that God created the world; that God loves them all the time; that Jesus was born, grew up, and died for their sins; that Jesus always loves them and is always with them; that they can ask Jesus to help them and forgive them; and that the Bible tells them how God wants them to live.

Eventually, Pentecostal children will also believe and experience the baptism in the Holy Spirit that God gives to fill our lives with more of His power. For the majority of children, however, most of the Pentecostal distinctives will be learned and experienced sometime after the preschool years.

The process described in the first two chapters of Acts is similar to the process of Pentecostal faith development in young children. In Acts 1:13,14 we read about those present in the room where God would first pour out the fullness of the Holy Spirit. We also learn, "They all joined together constantly in prayer." Since Jesus had just returned to heaven, the disciples and other followers were probably asking God to increase their faith and to show them what to do next. I believe that spiritual growth was occurring as a result of the disciples spending time in prayer. Then in Acts 2:1–4 the Holy Spirit is poured out on the people, and they all speak in other languages as the Spirit enables them. The Spirit gives the disciples increased power to be witnesses for Jesus. After being filled with the baptism of the Holy Spirit, for example, Peter stands and gives a sermon that influences 3,000 listeners to become Christians.

The development of Pentecostal faith and commitment in children seems to follow a similar pattern. Parents and teachers begin by nurturing faith in young children through prayer, Bible stories, loving relationships, and by good example. In addition, as children sit with parents in Pentecostal services, they begin to see examples of the work of the Holy Spirit during worship as God gives spiritual gifts of messages and interpretations, prophecy, healing, and words of wisdom or knowledge. Gradually, the children's understanding about and desire for God increases. At some point, God will add Pentecostal distinctives to children's growing faith.

When children's faith becomes "Pentecostal" is at the discretion of God and the Holy Spirit. Jesus did not send the infilling of the Spirit to His disciples while He was still on earth. When the time was right, God did send His Spirit. Parents and teachers can trust God's Spirit to move in children's lives at just the right time and in just the right way to add Pentecostal growth to their basic Christian beliefs.

With these basics of the seeds of faith in mind, let's examine some ways Christian teachers can nurture early spiritual growth in preschool children.

NURTURING FAITH

In talking about early spiritual development, we will define faith as "heartfelt attitudes of trust and love in God that result in obedience to Him."

The beginning of faith is a good example of how different early spiritual development looks from mature faith. Why? Because children who grow up in church generally learn to have faith in God's people first. Gradually, children transfer their faith from loving, trustworthy Christians they can see to faith in a loving, trustworthy God they can't see but do believe. In fact, I believe God intends that loving, trusting, obedient relationships with earthly parents and Christian teachers will lead to a loving, trusting, obedient relationship with himself—our Heavenly Father. God refers to this process in Ephesians 5:1, "Be imitators of God, therefore, as dearly loved children." This verse refers to the way a child imitates the people who love him. Little girls wear their mothers' perfume. Little boys push toy mowers behind their fathers while they mow their lawns. In the same way, children who learn to feel loved by God, will begin to imitate God. At church, children will begin by imitating teachers who love them. How do young children know a teacher loves them? The teacher acts happy to see them and talks to them in the church foyer as well as in the classroom. The teacher tries to help when they have a problem. The teacher plans ways to use clay, puzzles, paints, and other methods children enjoy as she teaches Bible lessons. If the child is sad, the teacher comforts him. If a child is excited, the teacher wants to hear why. Even when a child acts whiny, grumpy, or naughty the teacher still accepts the child and helps him find a better way to express his needs.

Does this kind of behavior sound a little like 1 Corinthians 13? If Christians who teach Bible lessons about God's love treat children with the kind of love described in 1 Corinthians, young children will also develop an "intuitive" idea of what God's love is like. First John 4:19 tells us we love God because He first loved us. In much the same way, children come to love grown-ups who love them first. For this reason, Christian teachers become examples of godly love for children. As children experience a teacher's love week after week at church, they come to depend on and trust in that love. When children love and trust God's people whom they can see, it becomes easier for them to love and trust their Heavenly Father whom they can't see.

How can parents and teachers know whether a child loves and trusts God's people? The early expressions of love and trust can sometimes be unusual and even humorous from an adult perspective. Consider two real-life examples.

One 3-year-old girl said she wanted to grow up to be a teddy bear, a chocolate chip cookie, or Pastor Wannenmacher—a fairly unexpected combination to say the least. And yet, from a child's perspective, the girl has given her pastor a high compliment and has expressed a hopeful sign of spiritual growth. Teddy bears and chocolate chip cookies are favorites of many young children. Teddy bears are soft and huggable and provide comfort in the dark or when a child is left in an unfamiliar setting. Chocolate chip cookies are sweet treats that give children pleasure. Pastor Wannenmacher has given enough loving attention to this little girl to become categorized right along with her other childhood favorites.

One Sunday, a 2-year-old boy named Brandon greeted his Sunday school teacher in a way that also demonstrated early spiritual development. When Brandon saw his teacher, he grinned, waved, and said, "Hi, Ch—!" After returning Brandon's greeting, the teacher asked his mother what the toddler had called her. The mother smiled and explained, "Well, he calls you 'Church.' Whenever I say, 'Come on, Brandon, we're going to church,' he thinks we're coming to see you." At first the teacher wondered if she should have given Brandon a name to call her, but then the spiritual significance of Brandon's greeting began to sink in. Brandon's concept of the church was accurate. The Bible says the church is not a building. God's people are the church. If this 2-year-old already loves and trusts one of God's people and thinks of her as the church, then his faith is emerging in a promising, if unexpected, way.

PRACTICING COMMITMENT

Spiritual commitment involves behavior: A committed person puts his faith into action. James 1:22 says, "Do not merely listen to the word.... Do what it says." Young children need to know God's Word with their minds, believe God's Word with their hearts, and begin doing God's Word in their lives. Before young children can live out God's Word in everyday settings however, they need to practice it at church. Children use practice to learn all their skills—talking, walking, riding a trike, learning to swim—all new activities take practice.

Practice is also needed for spiritual skills. Teachers who want to see children's commitment to God extend beyond the church walls need to provide practice opportunities during Bible lessons that will help children develop skills for living out their faith at home.

Hands-on learning in the early childhood Bible lesson is an effective form of this practice. If a teacher wants children to learn to help others at home, she should plan activities that allow children to practice helping others at church. If a teacher wants children to share during the week, he should plan activities that make it enjoyable and easy to share during the Bible lesson at church. As children's abilities begin to improve, the teacher should praise their efforts and tell them, "God is pleased when you share at church and at home."

Setting up hands-on learning activities that provide effective practice, takes insight and wisdom on the teacher's part. For example, many young children do not like to share. The teacher must use wisdom to set up sharing practice that the children will enjoy and accomplish with relative ease. For example, a teacher might ask two children to break a saltine cracker into fourths and divide it between the two of them, as Jesus broke the bread and fish into pieces to feed the multitude. In another lesson, a teacher might sort pieces of an animal puzzle among four children and help them work as a group to assemble one of the animals God created. In both cases, the teacher would be present to help children succeed, to help resolve disagreements, and to praise children for their efforts.

Teaching children to live committed Christian lives takes commitment on the teacher's part. Telling Bible stories is an important part of nurturing belief and faith in God. Most teachers know the kind of preparation required to tell Bible stories. Planning hands-on ways to practice commitment, however, calls for more preparation by teachers. And yet, if children are to be doers of the Word as well as hearers of the Word, they must be given opportunities to practice at church the skills they will need to live in biblical ways every day of the week.

Teachers who make this additional commitment can claim the promise of Galatians 6:9, "Let us not become weary in doing good, for at the proper time we will reap a harvest if we do not give up." Nurturing the seeds of commitment does take work, but God promises that our work will bring a harvest.

TEACHING PENTECOSTAL PRAYER

Learning to pray and having God answer prayers are important aspects of both faith and commitment.

Praying is talking with God. During the first years of life, children gradually learn to talk with their parents. Talking becomes a way to express and receive love from parents. During the first years of life, children can also learn to talk with their Heavenly Father. If children learn to pray comfortably and regularly during their preschool years, praying to God throughout their lives can become as natural as talking to people around them.

I'd recommend teaching young children to use prayer styles represented in the Bible by Daniel and David.

Daniel represents learning consistent prayer habits. "Three times a day he got down on his knees and prayed, giving thanks to his God" (Daniel 6:10). Daniel was so consistent with his prayer routines that his enemies depended on Daniel's prayer habits to incriminate him (Daniel 6:1–28). What was God's response to Daniel's prayer routines? "Daniel was lifted from the den, no wound was found on him, because he had trusted in his God" (Daniel 6:23). Daniel's routine of everyday prayer built his faith to trust God even in a lion's den.

Daniel organized everyday prayer habits. Teachers can begin to teach young children prayer habits too. Even 1-year-olds can learn to fold their hands and say "Amen!" at the end of prayers. Older preschoolers can learn and practice various "prayer postures"—bowing their heads, closing their eyes, and kneeling. Teachers can also help young children pick specific times to establish prayer habits, such as before eating, before sleeping, and before trips. These routine prayer times can be role-played in the home living center as the children pretend to put dolls to bed or to pray over pretend food they have shaped from clay. The prayer habits can also be used to take prayer requests during a regular prayer segment of a lesson or to pray before eating a snack.

I-say-you-say prayers can help children memorize some prayers or learn prayer patterns to use on regular occasions. To teach I-say-you-say prayers, a teacher says a prayer one small phrase at a time. The children repeat each phrase after the teacher. This method can be used to help children memorize rhyming prayers, such as "God is great, and God is good," or longer Bible prayers like "The Lord's Prayer." The same method can be used to introduce young children to the idea of talking to God with the same kinds of words used to talk with one another. Eventually, children will become comfortable saying a prayer without the teacher's help.

Art projects can provide another way to encourage prayers at regular times. At church, children can complete art projects related to praying at home. Perhaps children will make a prayer-related switch cover. Each time a child or parent turns off the bedroom light, he will be reminded to pray. Another project might be a decorated checklist that children and parents mark each time they pray for a week. While teachers cannot guarantee that such projects will be used at home, teachers can provide the projects and pray that the Holy Spirit will prompt children and parents to use them to establish prayer habits.

David represents a second prayer style young children can learn. The Psalms indicate David prayed at spontaneous moments throughout each day. In psalms that David wrote, he displayed the range of his prayers to God. When David was troubled and could not sleep, he talked to God (Psalm 4). When David sinned, he cried out in repentance to God (Psalm 51). When God delivered David from trouble, David returned thanks and sang of the goodness of God (Psalm 40). Even when David thought about his early life as a shepherd, he used it in a prayer (Psalm 23).

Teachers can introduce young children to spontaneous prayers in many ways. As a child touches a seashell or a kitten, the teacher can say a sentence-prayer thanking God for His creation. If a child skins his knee or bumps his head, the teacher can add praying to first-aid as a natural response to hurts. Teachers and children can create simple prayer songs that give praise to God while children play rhythm instruments or wave streamers in time to the music. After telling a Bible story that the children enjoyed, a teacher can ask volunteers to tell God what they liked about the story. These kinds of spontaneous, David-style prayers generally reflect the response of our hearts, or feelings, to God. The habitual, Daniel-style prayers generally reflect the submission of our wills to God as we make the conscious decision to pray. Children's spiritual growth will benefit from both the discipline of regular prayer habits and the heartfelt response of spontaneous prayers.

THE SPIRIT'S ROLE IN SPIRITUAL GROWTH

This chapter has suggested a few ways Christian teachers can nurture the beginnings of faith and commitment in young children. If you are interested in learning more about what you can do to help young children grow spiritually, read *Focus on Early Childhood*, available from Gospel Publishing House. This early childhood training handbook describes normal preschool behavior and gives specific strategies for nurturing early spiritual growth.

Christian teachers can play an important role in early spiritual growth, but it's even more important to remember the Lord's role in faith development. The Book of Acts describes the balance of what teachers do and what the Lord does. According to Acts, the Early Church "devoted themselves to the apostles' teaching and to the fellowship, to breaking of bread and to prayer.... And the Lord added to their number daily those who were being saved" (2:42,47). In the Great Commission, Jesus told His followers to go and make disciples. That's our part of the work—telling others about the wonders and love of God. However, the passage in Acts 2 makes it clear that it is the Lord who delves into the hearts of our listeners to convict them of their sins and to draw them to himself.

A children's church teacher told a story about a preschooler that shows the balance of our part and the Lord's part in spiritual growth. Her church used a bus ministry to reach unsaved children in their community. One child's comments during class gave the teacher clues about what the child's unsaved parents really thought about church. For example, one day the little girl said, "My parents smoke. Does that mean they're going to hell?" Week after week, the teacher gave patient, loving answers and continued to teach about Jesus' love and power.

One evening the girl's mother called the teacher. "I plan to be at church next week," the mother said. "Let me tell you why. Today I picked my daughter up from day-care as usual. As we drove home, a robin flew in front of the car, hit our windshield, and slid to the ground. My daughter burst into tears and said, 'Stop the car!' I didn't want to stop because I had seen some blood on the windshield and I knew the bird was dead, but my daughter was so upset that I decided it would be better to stop. When I pulled over to the curb, I explained that I was sad about the bird too, but the bird was dead. My daughter replied, 'Jesus can help the bird.' I was convinced that no one could help that bird; but to settle the issue, I walked with my daughter back to the bird. My daughter said a simple, little prayer over the bird, and the bird stood up and flew away. I saw it, and I believe it, so I'll be at church next Sunday."

The teacher's part was to keep teaching the Bible and loving the child. The Lord's part was to perform a miracle that the mother couldn't deny. Probably the Lord will never again perform that same miracle for another preschool child, but the Lord knows just what each child needs in order to come to a personal, lifesaving relationship with God. As you prepare and teach lessons, you can pray and believe that God will add to His church children He plans to adopt into His family.

8

Children
and
Pentecostal Faith

by Dick Gruber

Train a child in the way he should go, and when he is old he
will not turn from it (Proverbs 22:6).

This proverb gives direction to the teacher. He is to train a
child in the way he will go. What is that way? How can a teacher
be certain he is training him in it? To answer these questions
consider the time in history just after Joshua. "After that whole
generation had been gathered to their fathers, another generation grew up, who knew neither the Lord nor what he had done
for Israel" (Judges 2:10). These parents, teachers and leaders
did not know God, nor His works. The memorial of stones left at
the Jordan had become a forgotten symbol.

This same story could be told of us. If Pentecost is to be
accepted and thrive in the next generation, our children must
know God and His works. It is time to dust off our spiritual
memorials and show children the reality of a living Savior.

PENTECOSTAL FAITH IN CHILDREN

Pentecostal faith is developed in children through continued
exposure to the truth. Remember the story found in Matthew
chapter 21? Jesus had cleared the temple of the money chang-
ers. He was preaching to and healing people.

But when the chief priests and the teachers of the law saw the wonderful things He did and the children shouting in the temple area, "Hosanna to the Son of David," they were indignant. "Do you hear what these children are saying?" they asked him. "Yes," replied Jesus, "have you never read, 'From the lips of children and infants you have ordained praise'?" (Matthew 21:15,16).

Growing Faith

Children will grow in Pentecostal faith when (1) they are exposed to the spoken Word of God, and (2) they experience the power of God. Our children must know the Lord and the works He has done and can do in their lives today. The ideal place for this education is the Christian home. Cultural influences have created an atmosphere where Christian education of any kind in the home is in most cases only a good intention. A rise in divorce rates, a decline in the nuclear family, and an economy causing both parents to join the work force all serve to negate this godly ideal. So, the modern church has had to take a larger part in this training process.

Pentecostal Church, Teacher, and Curriculum

The church has become the primary trainer of Pentecostal faith. More specifically, agents of the church are models of Pentecostal faith to our boys and girls. The role of the Sunday school teacher has become extremely important.

Your role as a teacher of children is vital to the survival of Pentecostal faith. Your faithful enthusiasm concerning God and the things of God is required. Your steady presence as a teacher of the full gospel message is mandatory. Your willingness to build relationships with your students so they might see Jesus in you is paramount. Let's look at ways you can become more effective in transmitting this Pentecostal heritage.

Use a Pentecostal curriculum. *Radiant Life* is my curriculum of choice. It is written and edited by Spirit-filled believers. From the first draft of a lesson, care is taken to integrate the truth of Pentecostal faith. *Radiant Life,* with its scope and sequence, guides a child through systematic study of what we, as Pentecostals, believe. The message, eye appeal, and user friendly teacher's guide make *Radiant Life* your best option.

The Lesson, Life, and Anointing

Curriculum is like a recipe card. You are the Master's chef. Recipe cards were never meant to be served for Sunday dinner any more than curriculum was meant to be read to a class. If children are to taste and see that the Lord is good, then you must prepare that meal called the lesson. Add to it those things which will make it more palatable to the ones you serve.

The curriculum and the lesson that springs from it are not enough. You must be a Pentecostal believer. You must be a teacher who practices the presence of God. Your life in and out of the classroom, must be of dedication to the Lord and His children. The boys and girls of your class will learn by your life. Their Pentecostal faith will be caught rather than taught.

Does this mean that you only need to live as a Pentecostal in order to pass this heritage to the next generation? No. Your life, combined with your teaching, serve to present Pentecostal faith in a tangible way which children can emulate.

The Matthew 21 model includes both the teaching or preaching of the Word and the miraculous. Children are no longer satisfied with stories of a great past. The good old days are just that. Good and old. Children need to experience the power of God in their lives today. The lesson and life of the teacher must be joined by a third strand of anointing. The anointing of the Holy Spirit on your ministry is essential if Pentecostal faith is to be believed and practiced by the children.

Boys and girls must know that Jesus is not simply a historical or curriculum person. The children in Matthew 21 saw the good things Jesus did. When exposed to this, they naturally praised Him. Their praise wasn't confined to Pentecostal form or church traditions. They shouted praise in such a way as to make the church leaders uncomfortable.

A warning to you. Once the door of Pentecostal faith is opened to children, a flood of the miraculous will flow as has never been witnessed in your church before. Children will pray with profound faith. They will witness, and the supernatural will become an important part of everyday living.

James said it best when he penned, "In the same way, faith by itself, if it is not accompanied by action, is dead." (James 2:17). Elementary children are concrete thinkers. When a teacher says to "put feet to your faith," they wonder how it will fit in their shoes. If you tell a child that faith must be accompanied by action he will ask you how to act.

When a child experiences the power of God, he immediately wants to share the experience. A child who is trained in prayer believes that God really does hear and answer prayer. He may even become impatient when an immediate answer does not come forth. By the same token, a boy or girl who is not exposed to the power of God develops no hunger for this power. Tell a child God is dead, and he may just believe you are right. The Judges 2:10 generation grew up near to the power of God. Time and again their nation witnessed the miraculous hand of God both in guidance and deliverance. Perhaps the parents didn't want to expose the children to the cruelties of war. Maybe they thought it best to teach the children when they came to an appropriate age of understanding. Whatever the case, the heritage of faith and practice was not passed on.

The time has come to introduce your class to the realities of Pentecostal faith. When the record of your work on earth is exposed, it should read, "The teacher who raised a generation which knew the Lord and His mighty works."

THE HOLY SPIRIT

As Pentecostals, we hold distinctives which separate our movement from other holiness movements. The more prevalent of these is the baptism in the Holy Spirit with the initial physical evidence of speaking in unknown tongues. This most basic, yet important, distinctive must be taught to the children.

One day my daughter asked, "Dad, how are we different from the Baptists?" What followed was over an hour of questions and answers about God, His power, and Pentecost today. I often wish I had recorded that session. Her childlike questions mirror many that other children carry unanswered. Jesus said, "Let the little children come to me" (Matthew 19:14). Leading children into the baptism in the Holy Spirit is another opportunity for you to let children come to Jesus. As in any spiritual presentation which comes to a point of response, you are to let children find Jesus. Do not push nor drag them into this experience. The word "let" implies that the child, after receiving the facts, will naturally come to Jesus.

When presenting the baptism in the Holy Spirit, give children adequate time to ask questions, to talk among themselves, and come to Jesus when they are ready. The Holy Spirit is a perfect gentleman and as such would never force himself on others. Do not push children into this experience before they are ready.

Some of the boys and girls in your class will exhibit a sincere desire to receive this marvelous gift. Those that don't should not be made to feel they are second-class Christians, or less than spiritual. Let God be God! He will perform the work in the lives of boys and girls as they are ready to receive. Those that don't care to seek the Baptism should be encouraged to sit and observe or pray for friends who desire the gift.

While attending Bible college, I heard a teaching one day on the baptism in the Holy Spirit. The teaching was so simple that with little adaptation I have used it on numerous occasions when teaching children about the Holy Spirit. Since 1980 I have utilized this teaching in churches and camps. A high percentage of children in these sessions have received the gift of the Holy Spirit.

HOLY SPIRIT BAPTISM IS NOT...

I have discovered that when a child is properly instructed concerning this gift, he will easily be filled with the Spirit. We will begin with seven things that the baptism in the Holy Spirit is not.

Not the Same as Salvation

This is a unique, second gift God bestows upon believers. A prime example of this can be found in Acts 19:1–6. Paul explains the good news, those listening accept Christ, and are baptized in water. Paul then places his hands on them, and they are filled with the Holy Spirit. Being filled with the Holy Spirit and speaking in other tongues is not a requirement for a home in heaven. Anyone who calls on the name of the Lord will be saved. This experience is an offering of God's power to assist the believer in living a victorious life.

Not for Bible Times Only

Ask the class how many have been filled with the Spirit. A quick show of hands will point out to those who have not been filled that God still does this work today. Jesus is the same yesterday, today, and forever. He still baptizes people in His Holy Spirit. Boys and girls around the world have received this gift.

Not a Natural Experience

This is a supernatural gift. You cannot fill a child with the Holy Spirit. Jesus is the baptizer. He gives freely of His power. He gives the gift of tongues. This is not like Spanish class in high school. The child is not filled because he repeats or copies what another believer is saying or praying. Acts 2:4 says, "All of them were filled with the Holy Spirit and began to speak in other tongues as the Spirit enabled them." This enabling power comes from above.

Not an End

Being filled with the Holy Spirit does not mean you have arrived. Some children receive the gift of the Holy Spirit and then sit back as if to say, "I don't need to pray; I have it!" I have even watched as children at camp told friends all about the gift but failed to pray because they received it last year.

This experience does not signal the apex of Christian growth! Being filled with the Spirit means you are now empowered to tell the world about Jesus. If it were some kind of holier-than-thou sign of completion, there would be no Book of Acts. There would be no Church. The infilling of the Spirit signals a new beginning for the believer.

Not an Experience Where Tongues are Optional

Look at a bicycle. These things come with wheels. You can choose different styles, but without wheels a bike will not go too far. Without them a bike is a boring metal frame. With them it will carry you to new discoveries.

Tongues are not optional. When a child is filled with the Holy Spirit, he will speak with other tongues. His prayer language may or may not sound like any other. God is the baptizer. This prayer language is something the child can use every day as he talks with Jesus.

Not for Adults Only

"The promise is for you and your children and for all who are far off—for all whom the Lord our God will call" (Acts 2:39).

Even Peter on the Day of Pentecost recognized the intergenerational outpouring of God's Holy Spirit. Driving a car is one of the many things reserved for adults in this world we live in. We would never put a child behind the wheel. The baptism in the Holy Spirit is reserved for whosoever believeth and that includes children.

Not Scary

God will not do anything scary to one of His children. God does not give us a spirit of fear. He is perfect love, and perfect love casts out all fear. The Holy Spirit will neither suddenly start shaking the child's tongue nor take physical control from him. The spirit of the prophet is subject to the prophet. When a boy asks God to fill him with the Spirit, nothing scary will happen. The child may cry, laugh, feel something, or feel little. Don't worry; trust Jesus.

HOLY SPIRIT BAPTISM HELPS US...

What is the baptism in the Holy Spirit? The baptism in the Holy Spirit is a baptism of power: "But you will receive power when the Holy Spirit comes on you; and you will be my witnesses in Jerusalem, and in all Judea and Samaria, and to the ends of the earth" (Acts 1:8).

To Pray

Encourage children to use that prayer language every day. Would you lock your new birthday present in a closet and only use it once a year? No! If you received a bicycle for Christmas, would you hide it in the garage and only use it at Christmas time? No! You would use these gifts every chance you get. Likewise, use the gift of tongues every day. Pray for missionaries, pastors, family, and friends. Pray in the Spirit and with understanding. "Pray in the Spirit on all occasions with all kinds of prayers and requests. With this in mind, be alert and always keep on praying for all the saints" (Ephesians 6:18).

To Witness

Tongues is the initial physical evidence of the baptism in the Holy Spirit, but the reason we are filled is not just so that we can speak in other tongues. We are filled with the Spirit so that we can be witnesses. This power to witness is seen in the lives of the disciples. They were scared to witness until the Spirit came upon them. After this experience, they witnessed to anyone, anytime. Paul wrote: "Because our gospel came to you not simply with words, but also with power, with the Holy Spirit and with deep conviction" (1 Thessalonians 1:5).

To Live

"So I say, live by the Spirit, and you will not gratify the desires of the sinful nature" (Galatians 5:16). God knows that we need His power to stand up to the temptation in this world that we live in. The baptism in the Holy Spirit gives us that power, the power to resist the devil and live for God. Children need the power of God. Boys and girls are assaulted on every front by a very real enemy. It is important that God become very real to them before their teen years.

"We know that we live in him and he in us, because he has given us of his Spirit" (1 John 4:13).

HOW CAN WE RECEIVE THE HOLY SPIRIT?

So I say to you: Ask and it will be given to you; seek and you will find; knock and the door will be opened to you. For everyone who asks receives; he who seeks finds; and to him who knocks, the door will be opened. Which of you fathers, if your son asks for a fish, will give him a snake instead? Or if he asks for an egg, will give him a scorpion? If you then, though you are evil, know how to give good gifts to your children, how much more will your Father in heaven give the Holy Spirit to those who ask him! (Luke 11:9–13).

Ask

How much more will the Father in heaven give the Holy Spirit to those who ask? Encourage the children to ask God for this gift. Children are often concerned that the tongues they speak may be fake, or that their expression of tongues is something they have made up without God's help. Luke 11:13 seems pretty clear. God will not allow the sincere seeker to receive anything but the genuine experience.

Children can ask and be filled with the Spirit in the Sunday school classroom. Or, the child may ask and be filled in the car on the way home from piano lessons. Give children opportunity to ask for this indescribable gift.

Seek

Seek implies a deeper commitment than a quick request and answer. Some children will be filled immediately upon asking; others will seek God for a time. Encourage children to look for the gift. They should anticipate the time when God in His wisdom fills them with His Spirit.

Seeking can be described as a hunt or thorough search for the answer. Encourage your class to seek God. Encourage them to seek His good gifts.

Knock

The one who knocks steps out and puts action to his belief. This may involve spending much time in prayer. As a teacher you should never discourage a child who is honestly seeking God. Because of schedule you may close your response time before some of the children have received.

When closing I encourage children to keep seeking and knocking. I encourage the kids to leave class believing that God will fill them, to continue looking to Jesus for this gift, and yes, to knock on the doors of heaven until the answer comes. God is not in the business of disappointing children. The child who asks, seeks, and knocks will be filled.

What about the child who isn't filled? It is hard for a child to watch his friends receive from God but not received himself. Encourage every boy or girl who desires this gift. God will fill the child at the perfect time. He will make this a memorable and special experience. He works with each one of us in different ways. Children can and will be filled with the Holy Spirit. Do not shy away from lessons dealing with this subject.

PENTECOSTAL PRAYER

Face it! Modern Pentecostalism is a movement which began in a prayer meeting. From the early 1900s, we Pentecostals have been known as prayer warriors. Our churches have been known to hold all-night prayer meetings, prayer breakfasts, and to take our needs to prayer chains.

Children need to be raised with this emphasis on prayer. They cannot simply hear what has happened in our recent past. Boys and girls must experience the joy of praying. They must know that God answers the prayers of His saints regardless of their age.

Paul wrote, "In the same way, the Spirit helps us in our weakness. We do not know what we ought to pray for, but the Spirit himself intercedes for us with groans that words cannot express" (Romans 8:26).

The Pentecostal believer can pray in the Spirit with full knowledge that God's Spirit in union—with his own—is making intercession. Each week in our prayer time, I encourage children who have been filled with the Spirit to use their prayer language when interceding for friends. Children gravitate to the concrete, so keep a prayer journal, record requests, the date they were made, and the answer. Show this prayer record to the children often. A concrete reminder such as this will serve to excite children about prayer.

This, then, is how you should pray:

> Our Father in heaven, hallowed be your name, your kingdom come, your will be done on earth as it is in heaven. Give us today our daily bread. Forgive us our debts, as we also have forgiven our debtors. And lead us not into temptation, but deliver us from the evil one (Matthew 6:9–13).

Children do not always know what to pray or whom to pray for. Recited prayers such as the Lord's Prayer are appropriate in teaching children how to pray. There are many different kinds of ways to pray. "Pray in the Spirit on all occasions with all kinds of prayers and requests. With this in mind, be alert and always keep on praying for all the saints" (Ephesians 6:18).

Praying in our native language or in the language of the Spirit can be a rewarding and uplifting exercise. Time taken to pray is never wasted time. A teacher once complained that her students would interrupt the lesson each week with numerous requests. Finally, in her frustration she planned a prayer request time at the beginning of each class hour. This has become the most meaningful portion of her Sunday school class.

Let me encourage you to make prayer an important part of not only your lesson preparation, but of your lesson time. The importance you place on prayer will be remembered by your students.

PENTECOSTAL COMMITMENT

"His master replied, 'Well done, good and faithful servant! You have been faithful with a few things; I will put you in charge of many things. Come and share your master's happiness!'" (Matthew 25:21)

What is commitment but the result of faithfulness? Commitment to God is revealed through faithfulness in life, ministry, and prayer. The first and foremost method of teaching commitment to children is in your constant faithfulness. Children who experience your commitment firsthand will want to live such a life of commitment.

The Psalmist wrote, "Worship the Lord with gladness; come before him with joyful songs" (Psalm 100:2). In one version the word "worship" is translated "serve." There is no greater joy for the Pentecostal believer than that found in serving the Lord Jesus. The quickening of spirit that accompanies the Holy Spirit baptism energizes the believer for ministry. A place of ministry must be found if the believer is to be satisfied.

We are compelled like Peter was on the Day of Pentecost. Though he had denied his Lord three times, with the rush of mighty wind, he became a powerhouse of Christian ministry. Commitment is evidenced in your faithfulness to serve God in the classroom, in the church, and in the community.

In the Classroom

Be there before the first child arrives. Your presence week after week, year after year, suggests a commitment that goes beyond forced labor. Children will see you as an example of Christian commitment whom they can follow. Your attitude of spiritual calling is felt every time a child enters your class.

In the Church

Be there for every service. Occasionally teachers fall into a pattern of attending church only during their appointed service times. This not only limits your personal Christian growth, but reveals a less-than-faithful attitude. I heard a preacher say once: "The person who attends Sunday morning loves the church. The one who attends again Sunday evening loves the pastor. The faithful one who attends Sunday morning, evening, and midweek loves God." Your constant presence in the church building assures your students that you have a deep commitment to Jesus Christ.

In the Community

Children need to know that their Sunday school teachers are committed to Christ all day every day. It is no longer enough to put on the Christian life for Sundays and Wednesdays. Your commitment to visit the child, call him on the phone, and to be available to him are important components in training the child in the way he should go.

Since 1980 I have given each child I serve my phone number. They can call any time of the day or night. I want the kids to know that my commitment to them goes far beyond Sunday mornings. I want them to know that my commitment to Christ is a 24-hour-a-day life-style.

One little girl called for prayer when her cat ran away. Another called for assistance in baby-sitting. A boy called to tell me his checkup with the doctor had gone well. Requests and comments may seem trivial to you, but to the child who calls they are mountains unscalable. A girl called one morning to tell me that her best friend's dad had been killed in a car accident. A boy called concerned about an upcoming divorce. Children do not usually come to their worst point of crisis during the Sunday school hour. Your commitment to help them anytime teaches a Christlike stability that is needed in this unstable world.

Consider the ministry of Jesus. He lived a life of commitment to the lost and to the mission to which God the Father had given. The Bible says, "On hearing this, Jesus said to them, 'It is not the healthy who need a doctor, but the sick. I have not come to call the righteous, but sinners'" (Mark 2:17). Jesus came to seek and save that which was lost. He is the Good Shepherd committed to the care and feeding of His sheep. You must follow His example when you care for and feed your class. The lost children need a teacher who is committed to their best interests.

The ultimate example of commitment that we can follow is Christ's death on Calvary. He was so committed to completion of His God-ordained mission that He died to this end. Paul wrote concerning this mission, "Being found in appearance as a man, he humbled himself and became obedient to death—even death on a cross!" (Philippians 2:8). "'My food,' said Jesus, 'is to do the will of him who sent me and to finish his work'" (John 4:34). Let that be your heart cry—to do the will of Him who sent you. Your commitment to training children will reap eternal benefits.

CONCLUSION

Are you teaching Pentecostal faith, prayer, and commitment in the elementary area? Yes! You cannot afford to water down or reject portions of the gospel message because these are children. The elementary children of your church need the power of Pentecost in their lives. Their spiritual survival may very well depend on your approach to the topics discussed in this chapter.

Pentecostal faith is a needed virtue in our world today. Raising a generation of children who believe the whole Bible is essential to our survival as a movement. Teaching children about faith on a level they can understand will produce God's work in their lives. Giving them opportunity to act upon that faith will strengthen them for years to come. "Consequently, faith comes from hearing the message, and the message is heard through the word of Christ" (Romans 10:17).

Practicing a life of Pentecostal prayer can become a joy for the child. Being filled with the Holy Spirit and using that prayer language each day will give the child overcoming power. "I pray that out of his glorious riches he may strengthen you with power through his Spirit in your inner being" (Ephesians 3:16). Because of the wondrous work of God's spirit in our lives we can be 100 percent committed to Him. Pentecostal commitment should be more intense than that of those who do not walk in the fullness of His power. Jesus said, "From everyone who has been given much, much will be demanded; and from the one who has been entrusted with much, much more will be asked" (Luke 12:48).

I started this chapter talking about the Judges 2:10 generation. Our children need to know the Lord and the works He can do today. Give them Pentecost! Let them come to Jesus. He will perform the miraculous in their lives. God will do mighty deeds in your Sunday school classroom.

When you've been faithful in this and God has wrought the incredible, you can say to the children what Jesus said to the demoniac He had delivered. "'Return home and tell how much God has done for you.' So the man went away and told all over town how much Jesus had done for him" (Luke 8:39). The boys and girls of your class will return home and tell how much God has done for them. In years to come as your students become teachers, evangelists, pastors, and missionaries, they will look back to your classroom where Pentecost was real. They will look back to you, the teacher who believed and witnessed and lived a Pentecostal life.

9

Developing Dynamic Youth Disciples

by Glen Percifield

If the Holy Spirit is not allowed to actively direct the operation of the church by controlling the lives of its members, the church will have lost its dynamic.

—G. Raymond Carlson[16]

DECISIONS OF DESTINY

Robert Frost portrayed a typical decision of destiny: "Two roads diverged in a yellow wood, and sorry I could not travel both and be one traveler...." Deceptive messages of music, media, and movies manipulate teens and lure them to choose the delightful road to eternal destruction. Destiny-determining choices are usually clear. God or the world. Heavenly manna or man's materialism. Right or wrong. Sometimes choices are cloudy. Play basketball or join speech team. Join Bible Quiz or chorus. Teens need an internal Holy Spirit guidance system.

THE YOUTH CHALLENGE

Adults glamorize their teen years and forget their passages through turbulent, troublesome, and terrific times. Toys were put aside for tools. Inevitably, they returned to toys, abandoned tools, and drove adults to distraction. Coping with the Disneyland life-style is a challenge.

PENTECOSTAL FAITH
AND YOUTH SPIRITUAL FORMATION

The Distinctive Difference

Pentecostals believe the Holy Spirit makes a difference in spiritual formation. Following salvation, youth should seek the baptism in the Holy Spirit according to Acts 2:4. Teens advance to ministry gifts of the Spirit (1 Corinthians 12–14). Continuing evidence of spiritual maturity is the emergence of the fruit of the Spirit (Galatians 5:22,23). The Holy Spirit is expected to be the major power in a teenager's personal faith journey.

Personal Pentecost Required

The baptism in the Holy Spirit is a personal experience. Neither parents nor teachers can purchase it for their children or students. The youth teacher will guide, encourage, and assure.

The *1987 Assemblies of God Youth Survey* reported that over 51 percent of Assemblies of God youth are sure of their Holy Spirit baptism. Their understanding of the initial evidence shows that 31 percent are absolutely sure that speaking in tongues is the initial physical evidence of the Baptism, while 25 percent are fairly certain of this vital Bible truth. This means 75 percent need additional teaching and nearly 50 percent have not yet received this wonderful experience.

The same survey reports that 37 percent received their Holy Spirit baptism in regular church services, nearly 22 percent at camp, over 12 percent in a revival, nearly 5 percent at home, just over 4 percent in a youth service, over 2 percent in a children's service, almost 2 percent in Sunday school class, and 11 percent in other settings.[17]

Pentecostal Faith

This is a faith that transforms frightened, impotent, and confused Christians teenagers into powerful witnesses of the wonderful grace of God. Youth connect directly to God's awesome power. They deeply love God and demonstrate love to neighbors. They gain a new dimension and grasp of dynamic worship, anointed witnessing, good works, God's Word, and spiritual warfare. In essence they become more like Jesus Christ.

Initial Pentecostal Faith

Following salvation every youth should receive the baptism in the Holy Spirit. How can youth teachers facilitate this miraculous experience?

1. Be ready for every opportunity. A good Pentecostal Sunday School curriculum, like *Radiant Life Teen* and *Radiant Life HiTeen*, discusses the baptism in the Holy Spirit several times a year; however, teens are ready for this experience at unpredictable times. Three key passages point to the initial physical evidence of speaking in tongues as the Spirit gives the utterance (Acts 2:4; 10:45–47; 19:6). First, tongues were given at Pentecost. Second, tongues were given to the Gentiles. Third, tongues continued when additional believers were baptized at Ephesus.

2. Provide prayer opportunities whenever the Holy Spirit impresses you. Briefly explain how the Holy Spirit is leading, and then wait for yielded youth to respond.

3. Encourage Spirit-filled youth to pray with other youth. When teens minister to teens, both receive blessings. Always remember Jesus Christ is the baptizer.

4. Allow teens to share personal Pentecostal experiences. Testimonies may spark a revival. Let the fire fall! Fear is overcome when teens see friends receive this wonderful gift.

5. Assure youth that God answers earnest seekers. Luke 11:9–13 assures teens that God answers those who ask, seek, knock, and never give up. He gives good gifts, and He will "give the Holy Spirit to those who ask him"!

6. Emphasize God is ready right now. Some youth may need more learning. They may need to receive forgiveness. Or, they may simply need to completely surrender their lives to God. They must place their entire lives—past, present, and future—in the hands of the Baptizer, Jesus Christ.

7. Recognize God's sovereignty. We do not command God. We ask God! He knows everything; we know partially. God may have a better plan. Be positive with youth who are not baptized in the Holy Spirit and assure them God has everything under control. We obey and follow one step at a time.

FAITH DEVELOPMENT

Biblical Faith Basics

God gives everyone a measure of faith (Romans 12:3). The promise of the Spirit is received by faith (Galatians 3:14). Faith is one of the gifts of the Spirit (1 Corinthians 12:9). Faith is the substance of hope and evidence of the invisible (Hebrews 11:1). Some have little faith (Matthew 6:30). Some have great faith (Matthew 8:10). Some are full of faith (Acts 6:5). Faith can be increased (Luke 17:5; 2 Corinthians 10:15).

Faith Stages

This developmental concept, adapted from Kohlberg's moral development stages and Havighurst's developmental tasks, suggests that everyone from every religion climbs the same upward faith ladder one step at a time. Once advancing to the next stage, the individual does not return to a lower stage but may understand concepts found in the stage above. James Fowler suggests a six-stage spiritual formation ladder. When teens accept Christ for the first time, they may begin at stage one and develop through stage three. Rarely do teens advance beyond this stage.

Stage one: Preschoolers discover a magical or fantasy faith through actions, emotions, attitudes, and stories of closely related adults.

Stage two: Elementary children separate fact from fiction. True Bible facts and stories make a difference.

Stage three: Adolescents, increasing in mental ability and capacity for abstract theological concepts, view God as a close friend.

Stage four: Adults accept greater responsibility for faith. Religious rituals and activities must have meaning and reality.

Stage five: Middle adults gain the ability to see higher truth relationships between what appears to be contradictions.

Stage six: Mature Christians adopt an integrated Christian life-style.[18]

Substages of Adolescent Faith

R. Ben Marshall clarifies three faith positions for adolescents within stage three.

1. Junior high students (position one) see God as the heavenly Grandfather seated on a throne. In their opinion God does not directly affect them. They believe and confess for themselves but are usually unable to explain the beliefs of others. Their standing within peer groups is their priority.

2. Underclass high schoolers (position two) begin to interact with God on a more personal, helpful friend level. Truth is still filtered through significant peer relationships.

3. Upper-class high schoolers (position three) believe values and guiding principles originate in God. They develop a more responsive love for God, a desire for meaningful life, and an increased concern for others.[19]

Tree-Ring Faith

John Westerhoff III suggests that faith development is more like the growth of a tree. The rings of early growth remain as the faith circle expands. He suggests four rings of faith.

1. Experienced faith (preschool through elementary) is developed through events, exploration, testing, and reactions. Children adopt personal faith through observing, imitating, and interacting with people who love them.

2. Affiliative faith (adolescence) is based on group identification and is heavily influenced by music, movies, media, and interactive activities. Behavior and values are formed by the teenagers community (gang, clique, or friends).

3. Searching faith (late adolescence) requires answers to personal questions and doubt. Youth are vulnerable to both

cults and worthwhile causes. Wise teachers accept honest
doubts and help teens work out their beliefs based on the Bible.

4. Owned faith (adult) establishes full identification and
complete peace. Sharing faith is natural.[20]

A Biblical Pattern

Peter revealed a faith development pattern with promises.
Start with faith and add the following: *goodness, knowledge,
self-control, perseverance, godliness, brotherly kindness,* and
love. He said this takes effort, should be constantly increased,
and will keep you from being ineffective and unproductive. Also,
if you do these things, you will never fall (2 Peter 1:5–11).

RESULTS OF PENTECOSTAL FAITH

Powerful Witnessing

One characteristic of spiritually mature Christian youth is
that they are eager witnesses of the gospel. Empowered by the
Holy Spirit, teens want to share their wonderful discoveries
with friends, family, and their world.

Dynamic Worship

Youth worship takes on a deeper, more personal, and active
pattern. They do not worship identically, but all experience a
more profound relationship with their Heavenly Father.

Christian Service

Youth, when given opportunities, will participate in projects
to help both congregation and community. Ministry to others is
both a builder of faith and a consequence of increased faith.

Bible Appreciation

Youth develop a new appreciation for the Bible. They also
easily receive new biblical insights. They want to learn more
about God from His Word. They will not automatically appreciate boring teachers. Youth teachers must accurately and actively help youth discover the excitement revealed in the Bible.

Seven Faith Builders

An old commercial said, "Wonder Bread builds strong bodies 12 ways." Search Institute surveyed 150 congregations in each of 6 Christian denominations, analyzed the results, and discovered significant factors that increased youth faith.

Family Religiousness

Talking with mother and father about their faith, having family devotions, and helping others are the most important youth, faith-building activities. These were more effective than seeing parents attend church.

Family values and ministries can be encouraged and strengthened. Plan family ministry projects, social activities, prayer meetings, parent support groups, and family-to-family discipleship groups. Connect teens to a participating family if the teens' parents are not involved. Informal instruction on trips to the mall, recreational outings, and sitting around the family room is irreplaceable.

Encourage parents to demonstrate their Pentecostal beliefs. Suggest including teens in discussions about family tithing and offerings. Living out Christian manners should be part of work and play. Parents should support their pastor, youth group sponsors, and Sunday school teachers in word and deed. The more children see the real thing at home, the more they will appropriate the real thing in their own lives.

Christian Education Involvement And Exposure

Nothing works better than Sunday school to build faith, unless it is more of the same throughout the week. Increasing spiritual maturity of youth requires increasing their involvement in Christian education ministries. It's worth the cost.

Enrollment in Christian schools helps youth integrate their biblical faith in every subject. Christian teachers using Christian textbooks to teach Christian truths have an excellent probability of increasing Christian faith.

Well trained, highly motivated Christian teachers who are Holy Spirit anointed are the most effective. The Holy Spirit is our best teacher.

Church Involvement

1. Altar services and prayer build loyalty to both Christ and the local church. Youth praying with youth deepens healthy relationships and heals damaged ones. Leading someone to the Lord, experiencing miracles and seeing healings through personal prayer builds both excitement and commitment.

2. Church and Sunday schools are places for teens to actively minister. Teens make excellent nursery and children's church workers when they are trained and serve on a rotational basis (they also should be in the main service).

3. Teens should serve in visible ministry positions such as greeting people at the door, collecting the offering, serving Communion, and helping with water baptism services.

4. Special work days will help the church and church grounds look good and make involved teens feel good.

5. Special church board meetings once a quarter or twice a year could be designated for teen participation. They often have excellent ideas. Remember the wisdom of Jesus at the age of 12.

6. Involve teens in a wide variety of church ministries. Ask the Holy Spirit to direct you and receive His creativity.

Friend's Religiousness

1. Peer influence is a critical faith development factor. Promote positive Christian peer pressure.

2. Sunday school class is an excellent time to discuss significant religious issues. Be sure to include how to maintain Christian character in high school social settings.

3. Bible Quiz trips promote Christian friendships formed around the Word of God.

4. Unchurched teens should be invited to a variety of activities. Youth ministry and social activities should promote sharing of spiritual and scriptural attitudes and actions.

Caring Church Connection

1. Every teen in the church should have at least one adult other than his parents who will pray for him, go out of his way to get to know him, and demonstrate he really cares.

2. Every teen should get to know the pastor. Sunday school teachers and youth group sponsors should invite the pastor and his wife to share their vision for the church with the youth.

3. Churches need to integrate teens, not isolate them. Time and money should be devoted to this goal.

Non-Church Religious Activities

1. Attendance at Christian concerts can be influential.

2. Participating in community- or school-based Christian youth groups impacts lives. Form a Youth Alive group in your community.

3. Plan community youth prayer projects and participate in national ones like the "See You At The Pole" prayer project.

4. A missions trip creates special bonds of friendship, teaches evangelism, and builds the kingdom of God.

5. Be creative with spiritual retreats and other religious activities outside the church building.

Service Projects

1. Christian teens can make an effort to help their community in the name of Jesus. This can include anything from helping with a blood drive to a community clean-up campaign.

2. A Christian youth service corps could identify ministry needs and meet them. This could include helping an invalid or elderly person around the house or providing baby-sitting or big brothers/sisters for single-parent homes.

3. Providing a homework helpers club for younger children could be a great service.

4. Supporting baby adoption and homes for expectant teens is an excellent service project as a pro-life statement.

5. Develop modern day applications of the lesson taught by Jesus when He washed His disciples' feet.

Creative application of these seven faith builders will develop congregational and denominational loyalty while helping youth develop habits of highly effective Christians.

PENTECOSTAL YOUTH COMMITMENT

Increasing both the quality and quantity of Spirit anointed Christian education will do more to promote Pentecostal commitment in our youth ministry programs than anything else we can do.

The Early Church

The commitment of Early Church believers included unselfish sharing, daily temple meetings, visiting in homes, and enjoying meals together. They carried out these activities in gladness and singleness of purpose, praising God and enjoying favor with all the people.

Pentecostal Commitment

Commitment is a vanishing characteristic today, even for adults. People change careers, political parties, families, communities, and churches with the same consideration given to choosing fashions or fast food restaurants. One of the most remarkable characteristics of God is that He never changes. He is the same yesterday, today, and forever. We are thankful that His mercy endures forever.

Five Loyalty Producing Climates

Search Institute identified additional Christian education factors that develop loyalty to congregation and denomination.

A Thinking Climate

Loyalty to a church is developed when the church challenges the thinking of youth and encourages them to ask tough questions. Difficult questions never bothered Jesus. With study and the assistance of the Holy Spirit, youth teachers can answer questions according to the Scriptures and the power of God.

A Warm And Caring Climate

The building, furnishings, and decorations should be warm and inviting in the church and especially in the youth Sunday school and youth group meeting areas. Remember to give your rooms a youth look. Let youth decorate it themselves.

An Inclusive Not Exclusive Climate

Every youth is invited to join conversations and post-church activities. Every young person feels as if he belongs and is able to make close friends among the group. Youth must be assimilated into the entire church. Youth teachers must constantly make this a priority matter in their teaching.

A Servant Climate

The congregation is involved in service to others. The church helps youth get involved in helping those in need within the congregation. Further, the congregation provides a way to help people in the community. Also, the church is active in providing for the poor and hungry, community services, peacemaking, and social justice; and demonstrates real love and compassion.

A Spiritually Uplifting Worship Climate

Lively worship is an integral part of a Pentecostal service. While everything is done in decency and order, it also is carried out with enthusiasm and energy. Church is not a place for a nap.

Recipe to Build Loyalty

With the right support Christian education effectiveness can be greatly enhanced. Christian education in too many congregations is a tired enterprise in need of reform. Often out-of-touch with adult and adolescent needs, it experiences increasing difficulty in finding and motivating volunteers, faces general disinterest among its "clients," and employs modes and procedures that have changed little over time. Pentecostal Christian education ingredients and methods can make a difference in building youth commitment to the congregation.

Start With A Clear Pentecostal Mission

Youth ministry flourishes when people and procedures know and agree with the mission. Learning objectives and goals should be developed, accepted, written, communicated regularly, and carried out by every youth ministry within the church. Include Pentecostal distinctives and base it on the threefold mission of the church—worship, discipleship, and evangelism.

Include One Involved Pentecostal Pastor

Effective pastors demonstrate a strong commitment to youth education, devote time to the youth program, and know educational theory and practice of Christian education for adolescents.

Add Spiritually Mature Pentecostal Teachers

Highly effective teachers rank high in mature faith, care about their students, and know both educational theory and methods that work for youth. Only about 40 percent of youth teachers demonstrate integrated faith. We have work to do. Most elementary and youth teachers have not developed an integrated faith.

Add Powerful Pentecostal Processes

The effective Christian education process provides intergenerational contact, gains spiritual insight from life experiences, creates a sense of community values, encourages the natural unfolding of faith, recognizes the uniqueness of each person's faith journey, encourages independent thinking, is open to questions, and helps youth apply faith to daily decisions.

Blend In Solid Pentecostal Content

The Christian educational content includes: Bible doctrine and information, core theological concepts, questions of human sexuality, alcohol/drug abuse, youth service projects, moral values, moral decision making, study of poverty and hunger, friendship principles, and concern for people.

Mix Positive Pentecostal Peers And Parents

The effective Christian education ministry actively involves a large percentage of upperclassmen and includes parents in program decisions and planning.

PRAYER PROVIDES FUEL FOR THE FIRE

"I will pray with the Spirit, and I will pray in the understanding also..." (1 Corinthians 14:15, KJV). One conclusion of the 1987 Assemblies of God Youth Survey was that youth who had personal devotions were out in front of youth in almost every positive category. A Pentecostal prayer perspective promotes profitable prayers.

God Answers Our Prayers

Youth need to be convinced through practice that God answers our prayers. Scripture contains many promises that God desires to say yes to our prayers. Of course prayers must follow biblical patterns. What are the guidelines for answered prayer? Larry Christenson identified five keys to answered prayer in his book, *The Renewed Mind* (Minneapolis, Minnesota, Bethany Fellowship, 1974).

1. Think God's thoughts. We can have the mind of Christ. We saturate our minds with the Word of God. The more we meditate on His Word, the more we think like He does.

2. Feel God's emotions. David is described as a man after God's own heart. The Psalms display David's depths of emotion. Fervent prayer and Elijah's emotions are mentioned by James.

3. Desire God's plan. Psalm 37 provides three guiding attitudes: trust God, delight in Him, and commit to Him. Then He grants our heart's desires. God's Word is a lamp and light.

4. Speak God's words. Pray the great prayers of the Bible. Start with "The Lord's Prayer." Learn how these prayer principles apply to daily lives. Pray other Bible prayers and promises as part of your regular prayer pattern.

5. *Do God's works.* If youth need to develop one behavioral pattern, it is obedience. Youth mistakenly think that freedom means, "Do what you want when you want." Real freedom comes through slavery to Jesus Christ. This bondage grants true freedom for a meaningful life, answered prayers, and eternal rewards. The old hymn, "Trust and Obey," may need a contemporary melody and rhythm, but the words are eternally valid for every age level. When we are willing to do what God commands, we will know what He wants.

Pray in the Name of Jesus!

Finally, we should do everything in the name of Jesus. We advance His kingdom with His authority. In the name of Jesus, demons flee. In the name of Jesus, sickness is healed. In the name of Jesus, the blind see. In the name of Jesus, the dead are raised to life.

Youth teachers should help youth gain spiritual maturity, increase loyalty to their congregation, and pray with confidence. They will become dynamic disciples!

10

Adult
Spiritual Development
and Christian Education

by William P. Campbell

Immature adults! Sounds like a contradiction, but it is not.
We understand that maturity—other than physical maturity—
does not come automatically with time. A person may be
physically mature, but developmentally immature in other
areas: emotionally, socially, mentally, and spiritually. Spiritual
maturity is of special concern to Christian educators, who like
Epaphras work and pray that adults "may stand firm in all the
will of God, mature and fully assured" (Colossians 4:12). Sunday
school teachers should exhort adult students with this charge:

> We must try to become mature and start thinking about
> more than just the basic things we were taught about Christ
> (Hebrews 6:1, Contemporary English Version).

James wrote to adults of the Early Church, "Perseverance
must finish its work so that you may be mature and complete,
not lacking anything" (1:4). Mature and complete, not lacking
anything—that is what Christian education is all about.

How can Christian educators promote spiritual maturity in
adults? What do teachers need to do and understand in order to
assist adults in their spiritual formation?

In this chapter, we will address the following questions:

- By what criteria do we measure spiritual maturity?
- What does the spiritual growth process look like?

- How does the teacher-student relationship relate to the spiritual growth process?
- How is spiritual growth impacted by the stages and transitions of adulthood?
- How can the teacher make the classroom experience conducive to spiritual growth?

OUR GOAL—SPIRITUAL MATURITY

Maturity summarizes the biblical goal of teaching. Maturity is defined in Ephesians 4:13 as "attaining to the whole measure of the fullness of Christ." But when you look at your students, how do you measure maturity? What yardstick can we use to track spiritual growth? Michael Lawson suggests four scriptural themes that summarize the idea of biblical maturity.[21]

Love

Jesus said: "'Love the Lord your God with all your heart and with all your soul and with all your mind.' This is the first and greatest commandment. And the second is like it: 'Love your neighbor as yourself'" (Matthew 22:37–39). The command to love ties together a great deal of the New Testament and Christ's teachings. It is the preeminent characteristic of the Spirit-filled life: The fruit of the Spirit is love. It is the quality Jesus said would most identify us as His students.

> By this all men will know that you are my disciples, if you love one another (John 13:35).

Teaching is to produce love in the student's life. "What is love?" is answered in behavioral terms in 1 Corinthians 13. Spiritual maturity is evidenced to the degree an adult exhibits Christlike love in all of life's roles and relationships.

Morality

"Solid food is for the mature, who by constant use have trained themselves to distinguish good from evil" (Hebrews 5:14). The mature Christian is (1) able to take "solid food," and

(2) able to distinguish between good and evil because he has developed his moral senses. We have not reached the goal of adult Christian education until adults are consistently making correct moral choices. The ideas of "constant use" and "training" imply a process. Spiritual maturity is evidenced by a growing morality and the skill and ability to distinguish what is consistent and inconsistent with God's will.

Theological Stability

> Then we will no longer be infants, tossed back and forth by the waves, and blown here and there by every wind of teaching and by the cunning and craftiness of men in their deceitful scheming (Ephesians 4:14).

Theological stability is both a result of and measurement of spiritual maturity. This coincides with Hebrews 5:14 which suggests that mature believers are able to digest solid food. Paul also makes this point in 1 Corinthians 3:1,2: "Brothers, I could not address you as spiritual but as worldly—mere infants in Christ. I gave you milk, not solid food, for you were not yet ready for it. Indeed, you are still not ready."

Christian Service

Teachers are to assist in the preparation of God's people for "works of service, so that the body of Christ may be built up" (Ephesians 4:12). Christian service is a by-product of Christian education; we are taught to serve. Willingness to serve the church in "works of service" is evidence of growing spiritual maturity. Adult Christian education helps people to discover their God-given gifts and to use them in meaningful service.

THE SPIRITUAL GROWTH PROCESS

> I urge you, brothers, in view of God's mercy, to offer your bodies as living sacrifices, holy and pleasing to God—this is your spiritual act of worship. Do not conform any longer to the pattern of this world, but be transformed by the renew-

ing of your mind. Then you will be able to test and approve what God's will is—his good, pleasing and perfect will (Romans 12:1,2).

Spiritual growth is the continuous process of renouncing "the pattern of this world" as a model of thought and behavior and allowing God to transform us "by the renewing of our mind." It takes place through the work of the indwelling Holy Spirit as the individual makes conscious use of his will and his mind.

Learning and spiritual growth, while not the same, do go hand in hand. Colossians 1:9,10 helps us to see the relationship between learning and spiritual growth. It has been referred to as the Colossians cycle because it points out the ongoing and cyclical process of spiritual growth.

> We have not stopped praying for you and asking God to fill you with the knowledge of his will through all spiritual wisdom and understanding. And we pray this in order that you may live a life worthy of the Lord and may please him in every way: bearing fruit in every good work, growing in the knowledge of God (Colossians 1:9,10).

The cycle of spiritual growth is outlined in five steps:

1. Bible—*"Knowledge of what God has willed."* Our teaching starts with God's Word. This is where students gain the knowledge they need to begin the process.

2. Life-implications—*"Spiritual wisdom and understanding."* Here the Spirit illuminates the mind to see the personal implications of God's truth. The teacher plays a critical role in this as he relates God's Word to the adult's life experience. He is answering the adult's question of "So what?" about the lesson.

3. Response—*"Live a life worthy of the Lord."* Here the student acts upon his new understanding of God's will; he begins to obey.

> Therefore everyone who hears these words of mine and puts them into practice is like a wise man who built his house on the rock. The rain came down, the streams rose, and the winds blew and beat against that house; yet it did not fall, because it had its foundation on the rock (Matthew 7:24,25).

4. Fruit—"Bearing fruit in every good work." This fruit is the practical benefit of living in harmony with God. It includes the Holy Spirit reproducing His character within us evidenced by the fruit of the Spirit (Galatians 5:22,23). Fruitfulness is also reflected in Christian service and a Christian life-style.

5. Knowing God better—"Increasing in the knowledge of God." Life in Christ brings a growing personal knowledge of God. We have progressed from knowing about Him to knowing Him. Of course, this brings further insights into God's Word, thus restarting the cycle. This explains the common experience of reading a familiar portion of the Bible and suddenly perceiving truths and insights we had never seen before.

The Teacher and the Learning Process

Just as a spark is needed for gasoline and air to explode thereby moving a car forward, so the role of the teacher is to bring a "spark" between God's Word and the student. Spiritual growth begins with God's Word. The teacher is to lead an adult from his present level of spiritual maturity to a deeper understanding of God's Word and how it applies to the adult's life.

The teacher's life and character—how the student perceives him as an individual—has a significant influence. How you relate personally (person to person) is as influential as how you relate positionally (teacher to student). Teachers can enhance the relationship by getting to know each adult individually. Keep a student file containing vital information about family, occupation, spiritual history, church and community activities, hobbies, interests, and talents. Personal contacts outside the classroom also build the relationship. In a sense, you are a pastor or shepherd to your students. Your responsibilities to them are much like your pastor's responsibilities to the congregation. Your students need similar care from you.

The Holy Spirit and the Learning Process

God's role in the teaching ministry can be distorted two ways. One is to discount it, saying God has nothing to do with it. The other is to make God's role a magical thing, demanding that God work against all natural processes or participation by man. However, the apostle Paul recognized a wonderful and mysterious sharing of responsibility. He said, "I planted the seed, Apollos watered it, but God made it grow" (1 Corinthians 3:6). God's divine working accompanies human effort; it is not a substitute for it.

The teacher maintains a twofold dependency: a need for knowledgeable and skillful human effort, while yielding to and trusting in God's Spirit to accomplish the task. This requires teachers to seek the Spirit's help. The Spirit's anointing is His enablement to communicate truth effectively. The apostle Paul said of his teaching, "The Holy Spirit's power was in my words, proving to those who heard them that the message was from God" (1 Corinthians 2:4, TLB).

The Student and the Learning Process

Motivation is a key to learning; it is what brings changed behavior. It is important, therefore, to create an environment of relationships that cultivates a student's motivation. How is Christian education different from secular education? Unique content is part of it. But the unique context of loving relationships is what sets it apart (John 13:35). Love motivates and loving relationships enhance spiritual development. Adults attend church for the fellowship, caring, and support they can give and receive. Caring relationships are the setting for learning and spiritual growth.

STAGES AND TRANSITIONS OF ADULTHOOD

The Psalmist prayed, "Teach us to number our days aright, that we may gain a heart of wisdom" (Psalms 90:12). There is a wisdom that comes from "numbering our days," from looking at the process of life and what each phase is meant to accomplish in God's plan.

Adult years are filled with change. Teachers can help adults cope with life's changes and help them discover God's will. God wants life's transitions to be times of spiritual growth and fulfillment. The more a teacher understands the transitions of adulthood and the dynamics at work within those life stages, the better he can guide adults to appropriate learning and spiritual growth.

Transitions in the Adult Life

The most critical time an adult faces seems to be when he is making the transition from one stage of life to another, or when a person's normal life-style is disrupted by events that produce pain, discomfort, crisis, or change. Specific events that initiate these changes in our roles, relationships, routines, and assumptions are called "marker events" since they mark a transition from one phase of life to another.

Some transition events are anticipated and bring relatively little stress, such as getting married, becoming a parent, starting a new job, or retiring. Others are unanticipated and more stressful, such as major surgery, a car accident, losing a job, a divorce, or the death of one's spouse.

Transitions are crisis times. Adults can experience the full spectrum of emotions: joy, guilt, disappointment, anxiety, apprehension, or loss of self-esteem. They may struggle to keep their emotional, mental, or even spiritual balance. Prolonged times of stress may even bring physical illness. Even when not emotionally traumatic, transitions are still a crisis in the sense that these are turning points in life. According to Charles Sell,

> Life has moments when we are like a trapeze artist swinging high above the crowd. He stuns the audience by letting go of one bar to seize another. Between the bars, he is precariously afloat in midair. The audience gasps as he dangles on nothing but his fading momentum. His life depends on his ability to grab hold of the bar swinging toward him. Between the letting go and the grabbing on, there is no turning back...transitions are really life's most crucial places, leading to either renewal or ruin.[22]

Transitions can be times of doubt, frustration, fear, and uncertainty, all of which most of us would avoid if we could. Yet we should "consider it pure joy...whenever you face trials of

many kinds, because you know that the testing of your faith
develops perseverance. Perseverance must finish its work so
that you may be mature and complete, not lacking anything"
(James 1:2–4).

Some hidden blessings of transitions are:

- Transitions strip away false securities and can create
a renewed dependency on God.

- Transitions turn us to the Bible to evaluate goals and
priorities.

- Transitions can be times of starting over and refreshing stagnated routines.

- Transitions are an exercise in living by faith.

- Transitions are a time to learn that God is faithful.[23]

God allows teachers to share in His work of bringing abun-
dant life to His children. Apart from the wisdom and training we
receive from God's Word we would be unable to withstand the
enemy of our soul. As Jesus warned, "The thief comes only to
steal and kill and destroy; I have come that they may have life,
and have it to the full" (John 10:10). May our lives and our
teaching comfort adults with the truth that,

> No temptation [test, transition, or trial] has seized you
> except what is common to man. And God is faithful; he will
> not let you be tempted beyond what you can bear. But when
> you are tempted, he will also provide a way out so that you
> can stand up under it (1 Corinthians 10:13).

Development of the Adult Inner Man

Many researchers have studied various aspects of human
development (see Chapter 2). One of these, Erik Erikson, has
made insightful observations on what he called ego or self-
development, which involves the development of inner values.
While Erikson did not consider the "inner man" as an evangelical Christian might use the term (Romans 7:22; Ephesians 3:16;
1 Peter 3:4); nevertheless, his analysis is helpful.

Erikson observed that in each stage of development an individual faces a crisis of tension between two inner values. A person's success in each stage of development depends on how he resolves this tension by his choices and behaviors. When the resolution is successful, a specific virtue emerges that blesses the individual and his world. Success in each stage leads to happiness while failure brings misery.

STAGE	TENSION – POLARITY	VIRTUE FROM SUCCESSFUL RESOLUTION
Early Adulthood	Intimacy vs. Isolation	Affiliation & Love
Middle Adulthood	Generativity vs. Stagnation	Production & Care
Late Adulthood	Integrity vs. Despair	Rich & Meaningful Life

Early Adulthood and Spiritual Development

Erikson's model views the early adult years as a crisis of tension between intimacy and isolation. The young adult, to be fulfilled and happy, needs to move toward the development of intimacy with others. Intimacy is defined as the ability to share oneself with others openly and without fear of ego damage. This is necessary to commit to others in friendship, in marriage, in work, or in any interpersonal relationship.

If a young adult does not move toward developing intimacy, he will move toward isolation. He will avoid situations that require learning intimacy skills. The result is isolation from others, a sense of alienation, and self-absorption. This failure to relate openly to others, and the resulting self-centeredness, has been noted as a cause behind the widespread abuse of drugs and promiscuity. Both are futile efforts to numb the sense of isolation.

Erikson's observations suggest that young adults need to develop the skills and capacity for intimacy, making interpersonal relationships a primary concern for young adults. Christian teachers can help adults understand that only in Christ can one find true acceptance and intimacy, first with God and then with others. Helping young adults walk with Christ enables them to develop the capacity for intimacy.

Intimacy can be thought of as a quality of relationship in which one can open one's self to another without fear of rejection or being hurt. The intimacy skills learned at this stage of adulthood impact other adult issues such as marriage, establishing a home, working relationships, and developing long-lasting friendships.

Many young adults suffer from feelings of loneliness. They have severed many adolescent associations in high school while also dealing with the harsh reality of life outside the "nest." New relationships may not yet have been formed. The pressures of setting up one's life—job, marriage, bills, new friends—are severe. These factors combine to make it difficult for an individual to feel needed. There are bound to be feelings of detachment.

The young adult who does not learn intimacy skills in relating to other adults will only compound this sense of personal isolation. Fear of being rejected or simply not having the self-confidence to open one's self to another will isolate a young adult from social relationships. Sadly, this can hinder the development of related skills and tasks throughout his adult years.

The young adult's spiritual life is closely related to developing relationship skills. They will benefit from the support and influence of other adults in the church setting. Teachers should work hard to develop an atmosphere of genuine acceptance in which young adults can explore and develop their relationships with God, themselves, and others. Remember, it is important for them to develop relationships, but intimacy with God is the essential foundation for developing intimacy with others.

Middle Adulthood and Spiritual Development

The middle-aged years, according to Erikson's research, are a conflict between tendencies toward generativity and stagnation, with an individual's choices and behaviors moving them in one direction or the other. Generativity means being productive in a general sense through creative pursuits in career, leisure time activities, child-rearing, teaching, caring, volunteer work, etc. It reflects an interest in helping to establish and to guide the next generation. A person exhibiting this inner value attaches meaning to life after his or her death. It is important to this person to contribute something that will outlive self.

Stagnation refers to preoccupation with one's own importance and being unable to make an investment in the lives of others. This individual tends to be egocentric, nonproductive, and self-indulgent. He may become depressed thinking he cannot contribute to others. Unfortunately, both this individual and those around him are losers. Adults gravitating toward stagnation are ill-prepared to face the closing years of life because they will have to deal with hardened selfishness, and will regret that little or nothing will outlive them.

Middle adults need to be developing an active concern for those around them, becoming productive and caring. Again, Christians understand that such altruistic qualities come from the new life one finds in Christ. God's Word and His indwelling Spirit produce the caring, self-giving life that contributes to the enrichment of others. As the apostle Paul said, "Christ's love compels us....Those who live should no longer live for themselves but for him who died for them and was raised again" (2 Corinthians 5:14,15). Christian adults, especially in their middle years, should "look not only to your own interests, but also to the interests of others" (Philippians 2:4).

Middle adults are the leaders of society, they pay the bills, raise the children, solve the problems, and provide leadership in the home, church, and community. Generally speaking, these have the potential of being the most productive and fruitful years of life. Therefore, it is important for teachers concerned about middle adult spiritual development to provide them with opportunities for service. Christian service leads to and is evidence of spiritual maturity. Help middle adults to understand precisely what are their spiritual gifts, natural talents, and what are the best avenues to use these within the church.

The middle adult years are also ones of testing and evaluation. Middle adults are testing the values regarding job, family, friends, spiritual life, and even the meaning of success. They are reevaluating who they are, what they have done compared with what they wanted to do, and whether or not they are accomplishing what is important to them. The Christian teacher of middle adults needs to be aware of these dynamics. With all the changes taking place in the middle years—perhaps even with disillusionment and a sense of disorientation—the teacher must guide middle adults to appreciate and depend upon the unchanging truths of God's Word. The teacher's challenge is to present the Bible in a way that is relevant to the middle adult life-stage. Take advantage of the teachable moments that accompany change and crisis to articulate the power of God's love.

Late Adulthood and Spiritual Development

Erikson presents the later years of adulthood as a conflict in tension between integrity and despair. Integrity refers to a sense that life has been productive and worthwhile, that one has managed to cope with life's triumphs as well as with its disappointments. Despite mistakes and some regrets, this individual is able to look back on life with general satisfaction. Life has been rich and meaningful. The fact that life is coming to a close, that he has spent his one-and-only life cycle, is accepted gracefully. Death is viewed as a natural event in his total life journey.

Despair characterizes the individual who has not successfully negotiated the stages of adult life. His choices and behaviors have brought him a sense of hopelessness and feelings of self-disgust. He is bitter over past failures. He anguishes in feelings of a wasted life. Valuable time has slipped away and not enough has been accomplished. There is despair that he won't have another chance. Death is feared because it eliminates forever all possibility of correcting past mistakes. These people die unhappy and unfulfilled.

Christians would agree with Erikson that the choices and behaviors of one's early- and middle-adult years will have consequences in later adulthood. Whether one ends his life in contentment and peace, or in despair and bitterness, will depend on how much of God's truth he has incorporated into life. The Bible contrasts the spiritually developing man—"He is like a tree planted by streams of water, which yields its fruit in season and whose leaf does not wither. Whatever he does prospers"—against the man whose values and behaviors have hindered spiritual growth—"They are like chaff that the wind blows away" (Psalm 1:3,4). The apostle Paul exemplified an adult who could look back on life, and forward to eternity with what Erikson called "integrity," when he said:

> I am already being poured out like a drink offering, and the time has come for my departure. I have fought the good fight, I have finished the race, I have kept the faith. Now there is in store for me the crown of righteousness, which the Lord, the righteous Judge, will award to me on that day—and not only to me, but also to all who have longed for his appearing (2 Timothy 4:6–8).

Retirement and changing health will likely induce a retrospective look as well as a forward look to what the future may hold. There will be adjustment to the death of loved ones, and the consequent reminder that one's life is drawing to a close. Yet this is also one of the greatest times to enjoy life and the freedoms brought by retirement.

The lack of activity and relaxed living may induce mental laziness, so it is important that the older adult continues to see himself as a learner. The latter years of life, even its crises, bring opportunities for learning and spiritual development. The older adult should seize all of life and live it to the fullest. The older adult can devote time to works of service and spiritual growth, to increasing his self-worth, and to building up the body of Christ. Older adults need fellowship with persons of their own age and opportunities for worship, in-depth Bible study, and service.

The spiritual maturity that comes with age is important. Many older adults have earned the reputations of being the pillars of the church. Their ability to pray, their experience in walking with the Lord, and their habit of faithful attendance at church provides an example and challenge to the rest of the church. Find or create ways to put their occupational, educational, and spiritual years of experience to good use. If the church provides the older adult with opportunities to develop new relationships, to develop new interests and hobbies, and to contribute to the work of the church, this time of life can be fruitful and rewarding.

INVOLVEMENT EXPERIENCES
FOR SPIRITUAL GROWTH

The teacher concerned with the spiritual development of his students will want to make the classroom experience one that will nurture and enrich each adult's spiritual formation. Perry Downs has identified four types of involvement experience vital to spiritual growth.[24] Teachers should strive to incorporate as many of these experiences as possible.

Interaction with the Content of the Word

Because Christianity is based on a faith that has content to be known, interaction with that content is essential to spiritual development. This is why the apostle Paul first prayed the Colossians would be "fill[ed]...with the knowledge of his will" so that then they might grow "in the knowledge of God" (Colossians 1:9,10). Paul instructed his readers so that they could be mature. Knowledge and maturity are not the same, but it is impossible for a person to be spiritually mature and yet be ignorant of spiritual truth.

In the classroom, use teaching methods and techniques that encourage interaction with the Word. The Bereans were reported to be of noble character because "they received the message with great eagerness and examined the Scriptures every day to see if what Paul said was true" (Acts 17:11). The teacher's ambition should not be to report what the Bible says, but to equip adults to use God's Word themselves as their personal guide to faith and conduct. Paul urged Timothy, "Do your best to present yourself to God as one approved, a workman who does not need to be ashamed and who correctly handles the word of truth" (2 Timothy 2:15). The teacher seeks to help this become true of his or her students.

Involvement in the Body of Christ

Like parts of the human body, the members of Christ's body are linked together. Paul made this point in 1 Corinthians 12, "The body is a unit, though it is made up of many parts; and though all its parts are many, they form one body. So it is with Christ.... Now you are the body of Christ, and each one of you is a part of it" (verses 12,27).

Spiritual growth is a process that takes place over time as a result of interaction with other Christians and participation in Christian service. In other words, the primary context for spiritual growth and learning is within the body of Christ. Without involvement in the fellowship of believers, adults cannot develop spiritually as they should.

Believers are not isolated; we influence one another and care for one another. The parts of Christ's body "should have equal concern for each other. If one part suffers, every part suffers with it; if one part is honored, every part rejoices with it." (1 Corinthians 12:25,26). Christian education must include opportunities for this type of interaction as part of its curriculum in order for Christ's church to be built up. "From him the whole body, joined and held together by every supporting ligament, grows and builds itself up in love, as each part does its work" (Ephesians 4:16).

Exposure to Models

Adults also need to be exposed to models of Christian maturity. This is part of the discipleship process. As we interact with more mature Christians, we observe and begin to adopt their attitudes and values. We see how they deal with the problems of life. In time, we become more and more like them. As Jesus said, "A student is not above his teacher, but everyone who is fully trained will be like his teacher" (Luke 6:40).

A teacher must be a model of an adult striving toward spiritual maturity. The study of exemplary Christian men and women, both from the Bible and church history, can inspire adults to follow their lead. In some way students must "see" examples of what the Bible is talking about. Concepts such as faith, love, and humility are hard to understand, but they come alive when we see them lived out in others.

Dialogue with Other Believers

Dialogue with other believers is the fourth type of involvement experience adults need for spiritual growth. Jesus had extensive conversations and dialogues with His disciples and others. Paul did the same. Dialogue was a major part of teaching in that time of history.

Modern study of adult learning also suggests that because adults are reasoning and thinking people, interaction is essential. Why then do we so often see teachers talking and students listening? Is true spiritual growth possible if someone only comes, listens, and leaves?

In the classroom, use teaching methods that allow adults to interact with the teacher and with each other. As adults share the wisdom they have gleaned from their life experiences, their struggles, and their victories, others are able to learn. They will change how they think, how they feel, and subsequently how they live. This is what learning is all about.

EPILOGUE

Thomas E. Trask
General Superintendent
Assemblies of God

A dying soldier asked the chaplain to write a letter to his former Sunday school teacher. "Tell her," the dying man said, "that I died a Christian because of what she taught me in her class. The warmth of her love and the tears in her eyes as she asked us to accept Jesus have stayed with me all these years. Let her know," he concluded, "that I'll meet her in heaven."

The message was sent. Some time later the chaplain received this reply:

"May God forgive me. Just last month I resigned my position and abandoned my Sunday school pupils because I felt my work had been fruitless. How I regret my impatience and lack of faith! I shall ask my pastor to let me go back to teaching. I have learned that when one sows for God, the reaping is both sure and blessed!"

Due to the nature of the office I have been called to fulfill, I spend much of my time preaching to groups of ministers, chairing meetings, and traveling to many churches. But nothing thrills me more than to spend time "one on one" encouraging a fellow Christian leader. So, if you would, I'd like to have a personal chat from my heart to yours.

Through the pages of this motivating book, you have been given ideas and techniques that can be drawn upon for years to come. But, as valuable as this book is, it is useless until you take these ideas and put them to work. These insights are now yours to invest in improving your relationship with others.

I feel deeply that the mark of Christian effectiveness and maturity is evidenced in relationships. We are not measured as dynamic Christians merely by the number of Bible verses we can quote, the number of times we attend church, or even by the amount we place in the offering, as vital as these things are. The true measure of a person's commitment is shown by the way he treats those closest to him.

First and foremost we must establish our relationship with God. No human connection can substitute for a growing relationship with Him. It is no accident that when Jesus called the Twelve, His primary purpose was that they "be with Him" (Mark 3:14). As the apostles preached with Pentecostal fire, it was noted even by their enemies, that they had "been with Jesus" (Acts 4:13). Before we can do anything *for* God, we must spend time *with* God.

Cultivating a relationship with God involves valleys as well as mountain top experiences. We may have to cross deserts as well as the green, lush plains. There are some who crave a "mentoring" relationship because they seek to learn the deep things of God without paying the price personally. Remember, someone else's experience can never serve as a substitute for your own.

Abraham was "the friend of God" (James 2:23, KJV) His intimacy with God was personal and profound. By contrast, his nephew Lot keyed off of Abraham's spirituality. Lot was deeply influenced by Abraham, but he was one step removed from the source of spiritual power. He did not build altars as a life-style as did his uncle Abraham. As a result, Lot influenced no one, not his neighbors, not even his own family.

Press in with God for yourself, at your own Pentecostal altar of prayer. Don't allow the insights and experiences of others to serve as the foundation for your walk with God. The heartbeat of the apostle Paul must be our heartbeat: "That I may know him" (Philippians 3:10, KJV).

How do you deepen your relationship with the Lord? May I suggest that you simply set aside a portion of your day to read God's Word and pray. Guard this time jealously and keep it as free from interruptions as possible. This time will create a spiritual hunger. Spiritual hunger is just the opposite of physical hunger. The more we eat physically, the more satisfied we become. But the more time we spend with God spiritually, the hungrier we become to spend even more time with Him. Spend time with God and you will eventually break through to glory, victory, and power.

I have also found it helpful to seek out at least one older and more seasoned believer to serve as a sounding board and an encourager. Every Christian needs at least one Paul in their life. The one we choose may not necessarily be smarter than us or more successful, but they have traveled further down the road and have a little more experience to draw on. They can help us successfully negotiate the many hazards in this life. There are pastors all around who can gratefully testify of the positive influence of an older minister who took them "under his wing" and helped them avoid embarrassment or solve problems that seemed impossible.

If there doesn't seem to be such a person available to you, some have found it helpful to glean from the models of the great preachers of the past through their writings. Men such as G. Campbell Morgan, Charles Spurgeon, Charles Finney, Smith Wigglesworth, to name only a few, have left a rich record of their ministry that will inspire as well as instruct.

In addition to a Paul, every Christian also needs at least one Barnabas. Barnabas was known in the Book of Acts as the "Son of Encouragement" (Acts 4:36). While a person from the previous generation may provide wise counsel, a Barnabas is someone of the same gender and the same generation. He or she is a friend who can joke with you, weep with you, call you to honest accountability, and encourage you. Some needlessly battle alone with discouragement because they refuse to share their burden with a concerned friend whom they trust. Blessed is the Christian who has a Barnabas!

Of course, all leaders need to invest their lives in the next generation. There will always be young Timothys who desire to be molded for effective use in the Kingdom. It is helpful to remember some of the struggles and questions of youth and provide encouragement, a listening ear, a generous portion of time, and a loving heart.

Yet, I'm convinced the most important gift we can give the next generation is a life of integrity. Remember, your reactions are being observed.

From the pages of history comes the story of a frontier preacher who took in a stray dog. The dog quickly became the family pet. The preacher's two sons were especially fond of the dog. The dog was as black as coal, except for three very distinctive white hairs on his tail.

Later, an ad appeared in the paper for a lost dog that fit the description of the stray, right down to the three white hairs. With the help of his boys, the preacher carefully plucked each of the white hairs. The owner, hearing that a dog fitting the description was at the preacher's farm, went looking for his pet.

The dog, seeing the man, showed every sign of recognizing him. When the apparent owner started to take the dog, the preacher asked, "Didn't you say your dog had three white hairs on his tail?" The owner looked and was unable to find the identifying hairs. He left without the dog. Later, a sadden father wrote of this incident, "I kept the dog, but lost my boys." The names of his two boys were Frank and Jesse James.

We teach and spread our influence in all our relationships, not only by what we say, but by what we do. I want to close this book with a poem that distills my heart in a few words:

I'd rather have example than precept any day:
I'd rather one would walk with me than merely show the way;
The eye's a better pupil and more willing than the ear,
Fine counsel is confusing, but example's always clear.
I soon can learn to do it if you let me see it done,
I can match your hands in action, but your tongue too fast may run.
The lectures you deliver may be very wise and true,
But I'd rather get my lessons by observing what you do;
I may not understand the high advice you give,
But there's no misunderstanding how you act and how you live.[25]

NOTES

[1] M. S. Peck, *The Road Less Traveled: A New Psychology Of Love, Traditional Values, And Spiritual Growth* (New York: Simon and Schuster, 1978), 44.

[2] Ray S. Anderson, *Minding God's Business* (Grand Rapids: Wm. B. Eerdmans Publishing Company, 1986), 3, 4.

[3] Thomas, Merton, *The Sign of Jonas* (London: Hollis and Carter, 1953) as quoted by Frank Bateman Stanger in *Spiritual Formation in the Local Church* (Grand Rapids: Francis Asbury Press, 1989), 64.

[4] Thomas, J. Peter and Robert H. Waterman, *In Search of Excellence* (New York: Warner Books, 1982), 280.

[5] Clinton, J. Robert, *The Making of a Leader* (Colorado Springs: NavPress, 1988), 44.

[6] Ibid., 32.

[7] Ibid., 22, 23.

[8] From message at the 1993 North Texas District Sunday School Convention, Waxahachie, Texas, March, 1993.

[9] Leith Anderson, *Dying for Change*, (Minneapolis, MN: Bethany House, 1990), 35.

[10] Steve Rexroat, *The Sunday School Spirit*, (Springfield, MO: Gospel Publishing House, 1970), 82.

[11] Keith Drury, "They Come For the Show But Refuse to Grow," *Discipleship!*, (Indianapolis: The Wesleyan Church International Center, July, 1993), 1.

[12] *DIRECTIONS For the Decade of Harvest Sunday School*, (Springfield, M0: Sunday School Dept., 1991), 3.

[13] Lyle E. Schaller, *Hey, That's Our Church* (Nashville: Abingdon, 1975), 147.

[14] Jim Walter, "Using Growth Principles in Adult Outreach" in *Reaching Adults Through the Sunday School*, ed. Larry Shotwell (Nashville: Convention Press, 1978), 47.

[15] Elton Trueblood, *The Company of the Committed* (New York: Harper and Row, 1961), 45.

[16] G. Raymond Carlson, "Perpetuator of the Pentecostal Heritage," Lee, Sylvia, ed. *The Holy Spirit in Christian Education*, (Springfield, MO: Gospel Publishing House, 1988), 134, 135.

[17] *1987 Assemblies of God Youth Survey*, 1445 Boonville Avenue, Springfield, MO 65802.

[18] Perry G. Downs, "Faith Shaping: Bringing Youth to Spiritual Maturity," Warren S. Benson and Mark H. Senter III, ed., *The Complete Book of Youth Ministry*, (Chicago, Moody Press, 1987), 51, 52.

[19] Ibid, 53.

[20] Ibid, 53, 54.

[21] Michael Lawson, *The Christian Educator's Handbook on Teaching* (Victor Books, 1988), 64,67.

[22] Charles Sell, Transition, *The Stages of Adult Life* (Chicago: Moody Press, 1985), xxi.

[23] Chris Caldwell, *Having To Deal With Transition*. Christian Single (published by The Sunday School Board of the Southern Baptist Convention; Nashville, Tenn.).

[24] Perry G. Downs, "The Curriculum of Adult Education," in *The Christian Education of Adults*, ed., Gilbert Peterson (Chicago: Moody Press, 1984), 118-121.

[25] John Maxwell, Injoy Ministries Tape Club. Used by permission.